THE CHALDEAN ORACLES

THE CHALDEAN ORACLES

Translated and Systematized with Comments
by

THE EDITORS OF

THE SHRINE OF WISDOM

THE SHRINE OF WISDOM
Fintry
Brook, Near Godalming
Surrey, England

MADE AND PRINTED IN GREAT BRITAIN BY
THE GARDEN CITY PRESS LIMITED
LETCHWORTH, HERTFORDSHIRE
SG6 1JS

Contents

Foreword

MODERN scholarship has established that the fragments known as "The Chaldean Oracles" embody the remains, which have come down to us in Greek, of a lost mystery poem, composed in hexameter verse in the usual style of oracular utterances.

The authenticity of these fragments is vouched for by numerous authorities, such as the Great Neoplatonists: Porphyry, Iamblichus, Syrianus, Proclus, Synesius, Damascius, Simplicius, Olympiodorus, Pletho, Psellus, Franciscus Patricius, Pico della Mirandola, Marsilio Ficino, and Thomas Taylor. Most of these philosophers have quoted the Oracles in their writings.

As Thomas Taylor observes: "They are not only venerable for their antiquity, but inestimably valuable for the unequalled sublimity of the doctrines they contain"—an opinion which was shared by the early Christian Fathers and the later Platonists.

The doctrines they contain have been attributed to Zoroaster, though which particular Zoroaster is not known. However, the precise details of their origin are not of primary importance, for in this they are like many of the most precious sacred scriptures known to the world.

It is possible they were called "Oracles" because they were handed on orally from generation to generation, like the early Druidic and other Mysteries, and were not originally intended to be written down. This would explain the reason for the nature and date of their origin being lost in the remote past.

In this translation by the Editors of "The Shrine of Wisdom", the known fragments have been collected and arranged in accordance with a Cosmological System upon which it is evident, from a comparison of the Orphic and Neoplatonic Teachings, that the Chaldean Mystery Poem was originally based. The more this System is studied, the more profound does its significance become for, as Thomas Taylor affirms, it reveals the source of some of Plato's most sublime conceptions, and, as a whole, is perfectly conformable with the Master Philosopher's most abstruse Teachings.

The material brought together in this book should prove of real interest and value to all serious students of the Ancient Mystery Teachings. Embedded, as it were, in these fragmentary Oracles, are the basic principles, not only of the highest philosophy, but likewise of spiritual Mysticism in its purest form. Their full significance may not be evident at first, but they will amply repay those readers who give them careful and thorough consideration and reflection.

'Philosophy is the purification and perfection of human life. It is the purification indeed from material irrationality and the mortal body; but the perfection, in consequence of being the resumption of our proper felicity, and a re-ascent to the Divine likeness. To effect these two is the province of Virtue and Truth; the former exterminating the inordination of the passions, and the latter introducing the Divine form to those who are naturally adapted to its reception.'
                                                                    Hierocles

I

The Primal Triad—Father, Power, Mind

In the Chaldean Wisdom the Absolute and Infinite ONE is
contemplated with profound silence as being wholly
beyond all human appellations or predicates. There seems
to be no attempt, in the Oracles themselves, to name That
Great ONE Who is absolutely Ineffable; but so lofty are
the conceptions concerning the First Triad, that this
silence regarding the Supreme is more eloquent than any
finite words could possibly be to produce that profound
reverential awe in which Deity should be approached.

The First Great Chaldean Triad is called:

> FATHER,
> POWER,
> MIND, or INTELLECT.

Psellus, in his Exposition of the Oracles of the Chal-
deans, says: "There is One Principle of all things, and this
they celebrate as the ONE and the GOOD. After this, they
venerate a certain Paternal Profundity, consisting of
Three Triads, but each Triad contains Father, Power, and
Intellect,"

The ONE and the GOOD are the Titles used by Plato to
denote the Absolute, but they do not actually appear in
any of the Oracles.

The FATHER is the Primary Intelligible One, the First
Conceivable One, the Original Revealer, the Ultimate
Principle of all that can ever be known, the End as well as
the Beginning of all that is or ever can be knowable or
intelligible.

POWER is the Principle according to which the Father manifests Himself—by which the ONE becomes TWO.

MIND, INTELLECT, or NOUS*, is Divine Prescience, or Fore-knowledge: It is That Which Knows with Divine Transcendence, and, by knowing, is the Cause that produces and provides for all that is made manifest or ever will be made manifest.

The Father is only to be known by and through Divine Intellect or Nous. When the intellect of man is empty or void of all conceptions that tend to separate him from God, then it becomes identified with the Divine Nous, and through this, ultimately, may arise to oneness with the Father, the Intelligible of all intelligibles.

I. "Not by vehemence mayst thou gain intellection of that Intelligible. All things, with the extended flame of the extended Intellect, mayst thou measure, save that Intelligible. Yet of This the intellection must thou gain. For if thou turnest thy Intellect in upon itself, without striving, that too shalt thou know; bringing a pure intent vision, thou shouldst extend the void intellect of thy Soul to the Intelligible, that thou mayst learn That Intelligible, since It subsisteth beyond Intellect."

This is the highest stage of contemplation, when the human consciousness is lost or merged in the Divine, by rising above the Intellect that knows and becoming united with that which is the End as well as the Origin of all Knowledge.

II. "Every Intellect (Nous) knoweth Deity intellectually, for Intellect is not without the Intelligible, and the Intelligible subsisteth not apart from Intellect."

---

* It should be noted that the words "Mind" and "Intellect", as equivalents of "Nous", are used in their original Greek sense and not the modern connotation. Thus, "Intellect" has a similar meaning to that conveyed by the present day use of "Spirit", and the word "Intellectual" has the modern sense of "Spiritual".

The Paternal Profundity is a Tri-unity, a Three-in-oneness, embracing (1) The Father, or the Intelligible One, (2) Power, and (3) Intellect, or Mind, or Nous; therefore Pure Intellect, in its highest subsistence, is one with the Intelligible. The Knower and the Knowable do not subsist apart in the Deeps of God.

III. "Power is with Them (Father and Intellect), but Intellect from Him."

POWER, as the Second Principle of the Chaldean Trinity, subsists between the FATHER and INTELLECT; therefore, It is united mystically with both. The Father is the unmanifested One, Who becomes manifested through Power, by means of Intellect; in this sense, Intellect is said to be "from Him", and yet, paradoxically, It is one with Him, even as the manifested in reality is one with the unmanifested.

IV. "There first is the Monad, where is the Paternal Monad."

A Monad is a subjective wholeness, which is one and yet comprehends and produces all numbers. The Father is the Paternal Monad, who is the Divine Unity or One from Whom all numbers proceed in an orderly but never-ending procession.

V. "The Monad is extended and begetteth the Two."

Thus, from the ONE comes the Two, from the Two comes the Three, and from the Three come all numbers and divine principles.

VI. "The Mind (Intellect) of the Father pronounced that all things should be threefold: His Will assented, and immediately all things were so divided."

The Duad plus the Monad equals the Triad, thus, simultaneously with the emanation of the Duad, the Triad is produced, and all things receive a threefold impress or differentiation.

VII. "For the Duad resideth with Him and gleameth with intellectual differentiations (having the power) to govern all things, and to give order to that which is in chaos."

The Duad—Power and Intellect—not only proceed from the Father, but also abide causally in Him, as the transcendent principles of all order.

VIII. "The Mind (Intellect) of the Eternal Father spake and the Three came forth, governing all things by Intellect."

The Father gives being or essence to all things, which enables them to exist; Power gives life or energy, which enables them to move and act; while Intellect guides them so that they move, or are moved with intelligence.

IX. "The Father immediately withdrew Himself, but held not back His Own Fire within His Intellectual Power."

The Father does not Himself proceed, but transcendentally abides, both in Himself and yet in all things, by means of His Fire, which is the Divine Immanent Spark in all things. But, in a mystical sense, His Intellectual Power also abides, for It is rooted in the Paternal Profundity.

X. "Such is That Intellect beyond, energizing before energy, for It came not forth, but abode in the Paternal Profundity, and in the innermost shrine with the God-nourishing Silence."

There are three aspects of each of the Principles of the Triad. From one point of view these may be regarded as the Abiding, Proceeding, and Returning.

Hence, there is an Abiding Intellect, as well as a Proceeding and a Returning Intellect.

In the superessential adytum of the Infinite all things abide in immutable Silence.

XI. "For the Father mingled every spirit from this Triad."

Nothing can exist or subsist on any plane or in any realm without the three principles represented by the Primal Triad.

XII. "For all things by these Three are governed. In Them all things subsist."

XIII. "For you may conceive that all things are subject to these Three Principles."

XIV. "(The Triad) measuring and bounding all things."

The First Principle of the Triad is the Beginning of all; the Second is the Middle; and the Third is the End, by which they are again connected to the Beginning. By the Father they abide; by Power they proceed; and by Intellect they return.

XV. "In every world shineth a Triad of which a Monad is the principle."

In every realm of existence and activity, the principles of the Primal Triad are repeated, and each subsequent Triad, in the Cosmological Scheme, is suspended, as it were, from a Monad in the realm above it; just as the First Triad may be said to be rooted in the Infinite ONE.

XVI. "For nothing imperfect revolveth from the Paternal Principle."

The Father is the Perfect ONE, and all His Works bear

the Seal of His Perfection, for imperfection cannot spring
from a Perfect Source.

XVII. "From the vortices of this Triad all things are
perpetually filled."

The Paternal Profundity is the Unfathomable Deep of
the Plenum, by the Power of Which all things are for ever
filled to the measure of their receptivity.

XVIII. "For the Intellect of the Father, Self-begotten,
comprehending His Works, sowed in all things the fire-
laden bond of love, that all things might remain ever
loving on, throughout the aeons of endless time, that the
diacosm of life might remain intellectually in the full light
of the Father, that the first principles of the Cosmos might
continue perpetually active in love."

The Father, Self-begotten, is the First-born Light and
the First-born Love: the Light which enlighteneth all
things, the Love which provides for them, and the Object
of aspiration of them all throughout all Eternity.

XIX. "Ye who know intellectually, know the Paternal
Profundity which transcends the Cosmos."

Intellect or Nous is the Higher Spiritual Mind, and not
the ordinary finite human mind. When this Divine Mind
is active in man, then his consciousness transcends time
and space, attaining to the real Knowledge of God.

XX. "That which Intellect saith, It saith intellectually."

As Thomas Taylor affirms:

"Intellect in energy, or in the act of knowing, is the same
with the object of intellection. For the object of its percep-
tion must reside in its essence, or it would perceive externally like sense, and thus would not behold the thing
itself, but only its image. But if that which is Intelligible is

seated in the essence of Intellect, it will in no respect differ from Intellect, for it will be essential to its nature, and will consequently be intellectual as well as intelligible."

XXI. "And of that Intellect which guides the Empyrean World."

In the Chaldean System the Empyrean World is the Subjective Realm as a whole, which embraces the principles of all that is made manifest in the Objective Cosmos.

'If God has an Infinite Essence, He must also have an Infinite Presence. He must be essentially everywhere, and if He be essentially present in all places, then He must also be essentially with all creatures; consequently, with the Soul of man.'

John Norris

'The simple, absolute, and unchangeable mysteries of heavenly Truth lie hidden in the dazzling obscurity of the secret Silence, outshining all brilliance with the intensity of their darkness, and surcharging our blinded intellects with the utterly impalpable and invisible fairness of glories which exceed all beauty.'

Dionysius the Areopagite

II

The Archetypal Ideas

A MOST important aspect of the Chaldean Mystery Teaching is that which deals with the Doctrine of Ideas. It is not one that is easily to be understood, for the very reason that these Ideas are abstract, noumenal, and universal principles, the significance of which cannot be fully grasped by the ordinary finite lower mind, which is only able with great difficulty to apprehend that which is abstract and noumenal.

These Ideas, as taught in the Platonic Philosophy, are the archetypes of all that is made manifest in the Great Cosmos, and, as such, may in a mystical sense be compared with the Thoughts of the Father.

XXII. "The Mind of the Father burst thunderously forth, conceiving with His transcendent Will Omniform Ideas. Winging from one source they leapt forth. For from the Father was both the Will and the End. But they were differentiated, being made participable by intellectual fire to other intellectual natures. For the King set before the multiform Cosmos an incorruptible intellectual type, and when the pattern of its form was impressed upon the chaos, thereafter the Cosmos appeared, rejoicing with all-various Ideas whose source is one. From it, thunder forth other ideas in unimaginable distribution, separated among the bodies of the Cosmos, borne like swarms of bees about the awful depths. Hither and thither, around and about they whirl, illimitably, intellectual thoughts from

the Paternal Fountain, mightily plucking the Flower of
the Fire at the height of sleepless time. The self-perfect
Source of the Father primordially welled forth these
Ideas, the original causes."

This is the most profound as well as the longest fragment of the Oracles that has been preserved.

The Mind, of Nous, of the Father, Who is the Primary
Intelligible One, the Original Revealer and the Ultimate
Principle of All, wills that all things shall come into being,
and immediately the Great Word or Name is sounded over
the primeval deep in which are conceived the germs of all
that is to be made manifest. From this Paternal Deep the
omniform Ideas leap forth, as from one inexhaustible
fountain. They emerge like the Thoughts of the Father as
He thinks all things into being. And these thoughts,
although the causes of all form, are inconceivable and
noumenal to all beings. But they speed forth charged with
ineffable archetypal fire, prolific and all-productive, and
are received by the other Intellectual Natures or Creative
Principles, of whom the Demiurgus or Great Architect is
the King. He is the actual Creator Who receives the
Thoughts of the Father and gives them expression in the
worlds of form. Thus out of the chaos comes the Cosmos,
replete with all-various types, differentiated into every
conceivable aspect of existence, pregnant with creative
fire, flowing perpetually into and out of the realms of time
and space, from and to the Pyramid of Creation, the
Flower of the Fire at the Summit of Everlastingness, the
Height of Sleepless Time at the Mysterious Borders of
Eternity.

In the Chaldean Cosmology the Empyrean or Subjective
Realm is divided into three "Worlds" or planes. These
are:

(1) The Intelligible   The World of the Pa-
     (*Noetic*)   ternal Profundity, and

	the Causal Triad of FATHER, POWER, MIND.
(2) The Intelligible-Intellectual (*Noetic-noeric*)	The World of Ideas and the Archetypal Triad called: IYNGES, SYNOCHES, TELETARCHS.
(3) The Intellectual (*Noeric*)	The World of Intellectual Fountains, The Creative Fathers, and the Flower of the Creative Fire.

There is a correspondence and an intimate relation between the Three Subjective Worlds and the Causal Triad of Father, Power, Mind.

Thus the undifferentiated and noumenal Thoughts of the Father proceed from Him by His Power through the Archetypal World, where they become differentiated Ideas or Archetypes, into the Creative Fountains or Intellectual Fathers who reflect, as it were, the Mind of the Intelligible Father and receive the Ideas as the intellectual paradigms of all created things.

THE ARCHETYPAL TRIAD—IYNGES, SYNOCHES, TELETARCHS

The Iynges are the Starters, the Wheels, the Whirls, the Winged-Wheels, the Living Spheres, the Shriekers, who, in a mystical sense, whirl out in all directions and swirl in again, emitting sound, and setting the whole universe agoing.

The Synoches are the Binders, the Uniters, the Maintainers, the Connectors, the Holders-together, who follow the Iynges, as it were, uniting their outgoing and their ingoing whirlings, and producing subjective and differentiated wholenesses from that which is undefined and unlimited in the Iynges.

The Teletarchs are the Perfecters, the Enders, the Completers, who consummate the energies of the Synoches and give to Ideas their ultimate perfection and integrality, so that all things proceed from perfect archetypes or spiritual patterns.

The Iynges, Synoches, and Teletarchs are each threefold, and have aspects or reflections in the Empyrean, Aetherial, and Terrene Realms. They constitute a Triad of Triads in which are the perfect principles or types of all that is or ever can be made manifest. As Porphyry says:

XXIII. "The number of the ennead is divine, being composed of three triads, and preserves the highest principles of Theology, according to the Chaldean Philosophy."

The fragments that deal with the Iynges, Synoches, and Teletarchs are very incomplete, and those that are quoted in the works of the Neoplatonists are not given in the original form in which they appeared in the hexameter verse of the Mystery Poem. However, since their significance has evidently been preserved, they are quoted here.

The Iynges

In the Paternal Profundity, which is beyond the sphere of the Archetypal principles, and is symbolical of the Mystical Darkness which is before the Pavilions of the Infinite and Inconceivable ONE, are conceived the causal germs or occult essences of all things. From these causal seeds the Iynges become pregnant, and as they whirl forth into the Immensity of the Unknown that which is inconceivable becomes conceivable, the initial impulse is given to the Cosmic Scheme, and the unmanifested becomes manifested.

XXIV. "The Iynges conceived by the Father themselves also conceive, being impelled by ineffable counsels so to conceive."
Each Archetypal triad has an abiding, a proceeding, and a returning aspect; thus each triad, in terms of itself, not only supplies the principles whereby all things proceed into manifestation, but also the means whereby all beings are intimately related with the Great Source of All and thus enabled to return to Him.

XXV. "For not only do these three divine principles unfold and co-ordinate all things, but they are 'Guardians of the works' of the Father and of the One Mind, the Intelligible."

XXVI. "The Oracle calls the intelligible causes 'swift', and says that proceeding from the Father they flow swiftly again to Him."

Proclus, who preserves a large number of fragments, says:
XXVII. "The Order of the Iynges has a transmissive power of all things from the Intelligible into Matter, and again of all things into itself."
They represent the highest point of all possible attainment and dazzling perfection, as well as the initial impulse to manifest.

XXVIII. "Many be these, who ascend leaping into the Shining Worlds; and amongst them are three summits."
These are the three heights of the Iynges at the apex of the pyramid of the Archetypal Realm.

The Synoches

This Triad, as the Archetypal "whole-makers", as Damascius calls them, supply the principles of all integrality, and not only give unity to the Thoughts of the Father, but also are the means whereby all beings are united with Him, even although He is transcendentally exempt.

XXIX. "Containing all things connectedly in the one summit of His Own Hyparxis, He Himself, according to the Oracle, subsists wholly beyond."

The Infinite is beyond even the Highest Heaven: He is the Unapproachable, the Mystery of all Mysteries.

XXX. "The Oracles concerning the orders prior to Heaven, declare that they are ineffable, and add 'Be Silent, Thou who enterest the Mysteries'. "

According to the Orphic Theogony, Uranus or Heaven subsists with the Synoches, and Proclus tells us that the Poem was originally prefaced by the words: "Keep silence, thou who enterest the Mysteries."

The Synoches, as the Middle Triad, are especially characterized by the Power of the Father. Through them the Divine Ideas are dynamic in the highest sense of that term, and their Providential Energy is the expression of Divine Omnipotence.

XXXI. "He gave also to His fiery whirls the summits to guard, immingling in the Synoches the might of His own Strength."

The Synoches are connective of extremes, so that in the procession of Ideas from the innermost to the outermost, and from the uppermost to the nethermost, there is an intimate relation and a perfect order.

They supply the principles by which all things are interiorly united in one great indissoluble whole:

XXXII. "For all things subsist together in the Intelligible World."

The Synoches are also the original principle of the laws according to which external things are connected or held together—as a fragment of the Oracles evinces—

XXXIII. "But as many as serve the hylic Synoches."

For Hyle signifies the realms of precipitated existence, resulting from the union of form with matter, which is a Synochean activity.

The Teletarchs

Archetypal Ideas are perfect and do not depend upon any process, such as evolution, for their perfection; rather they constitute the ultimate perfect Ideals which are the goals of all endeavour. The Teletarchs, who are the triadic Perfecters of all perfectings, are the cause of the perfection of the Archetypal Ideas. If these Perfections did not really pre-subsist all existence there could be no perfect Ideals towards which all beings could aspire and to which they could ultimately attain.

The Teletarchs are especially characterized by the third aspect of the Paternal Profundity, that is: Mind or Nous or Intellect; therefore they are, in a special sense, Intelligible-and-at-the-same-time-Intellectual and comprehend, in an idealogical sense, the beginning-middle-end of all processions from and to Deity.

XXXIV. ". . . Into beginning and end and middle things by order of necessity."

The principle called Necessity belongs to the Archetypal Realm, because the Will of the Father having been "willed" must *be*, but it is perfect and best, and provides for every conceivable condition of existence, without subjecting the Father Himself to the Law of Necessity. And since the Will of the Father is Omnipotent

and absolutely Free, all his creatures may arise to Tele-
tarchic perfection and liberty, and transcend the Law of
Necessity by their absolute conformity to His Divine Will.

XXXV. "The Teletarchs are comprehended in the
Synoches."
The Synoches are connective of extremes and therefore
are all-embracing in terms of themselves; but the Tele-
tarchic Triad supply the principles whereby ends are
united to beginnings, and vice versa, hence they are the
ideal perfecters.

XXXVI. "This order is the principle of all participation."
Providential energy is all-pervading, and is adapted or
made participable by the Teletarchs to all beings according to the measure of their receptivity and perfective
union with supernal natures.

XXXVII. "The Intelligible is nourishment to that
which knoweth it."
And it is through the perfective power of this Triad that
secondary natures are initiated into a living Knowledge of
Eternal Realities, for they are intellectual as well as intelligible, and know as well as are known in their fullness.

XXXVIII. "But since of the intellectuals some are intelligible and intellectual 'which knowing are also
known', as the Oracles say."
In the measure that the Teletarchs are unfolded within
the consciousness, so the evidences of Divine Goodness,
Truth, and Beauty are seen and realized, even in the
realms of time and sense.

XXXIX. "For the Mind of the Father hath sown Symbols throughout the Cosmos, that Mind which conceiveth
the Intelligible and knoweth ineffable beauties."

These symbols are the ideas which the human mind extracts, as it were, by its contemplation of Nature and the Works of God, for all things bear witness to His marvellous Wisdom which is the Logos or Word by which they are called into existence, perpetually sustained, and perfected.

XL. "But a Venerable Name leaping with sleepless revolution into the worlds through the swift fiat of the Father."

The Name or Word which was with God and is God.

'Do not suppose that there is anyone so foolish as not to understand that there is only one Supreme God, Who has neither origin nor descent, the Sole and Almighty Creator of the whole of Nature. We adore, under the names of various deities, His powers spread throughout the universe, to preserve and uphold, for we are all ignorant of the true Name which belongs to Him; and it is thus that in offering a different homage to different attributes of the Divinity, man arrives at adoring Him in His entirety.'

Maximus the Grammarian.

III

The Sevenfold Creative Fire

EVEN as the Sun is a most fitting emblem of Deity, so Fire is a most appropriate symbol of Divine Creative Energy.

Fire resolves substances back to their primal elements, but it also fructifies and quickens them to new life under suitable conditions. All processes, whether of generation or corruption, are quickened by fire.

The nature of fire in the visible realms of sense bears an analogy with that of the Invisible Fire of the Intelligible Realms. The Oracles speak of the Creative World as "The Fiery World", and the Divine Creative Thoughts as "Intelligible Fire".

XLI. "Thoughts of the Father, Brightness aflame, pure Fire."

The thoughts of the Paternal Profundity are symbolized by the Divine Ideas of the Archetypal World which are comprehended by the Mind or Intellect of the Creator or Demiurgus, and, in Him, are the paradigmatic principles according to which all things in manifestation are produced.

XLII. "To the Intellectual Lightning Whirls of Intellectual Fire all things yield their service by the compelling Will of the Father."

XLIII. "All things are the progeny of one Fire."

The one visible Sun has a sevenfold aspect as expressed

in the seven colours of the one light, so likewise the One
Invisible Fire of the Creative World has a septenary
division. This is unfolded in the Chaldean Mysteries as
the Intellectual Hebdomad or the Seven Creative Principles, which are called the Intellectual or Noeric Fountains, the Creative Fathers, the Cosmagogoi or Leaders
of the Cosmos; these may be outlined as follows, together
with their corresponding names in the Orphic and
Platonic Systems:

(1) The First Creative Father, the Once Beyond, the
    Abiding Demiurgic or Creative Intellect, the Pure and
    Essential Intellect, the Summit of the Intellectuals,
    Kronos or Saturn.
(2) The Divine Life of Intellect, the Proceeding Creative
    Intellect, the Demiurgic Mother, the Fountain of
    Creative Life, Hecate, Cybele, or Rhea.
(3) The Second Creative Father, the Twice Beyond, the
    Productive Creative Intellect or Demiurgus proper,
    the Intellectual Intellect, Zeus or Jupiter.
(4) (5) (6) The Three Creative Root Words or Logoi, the
    Amiliktoi, the Powers of the Fire-Self, the Pure Gods,
    the Unalterable, the Undefiled, the Inflexible, the
    Curetes.
(7) The Separative Creative Intellect, the Flower of the
    Fire, Upezokus or Hypezokus, the Limit, the Fiery
    Wall of the Cosmos, Oceanus.

There are fragments of the Oracles which deal with
each of the above Seven Principles in mystical language
which becomes pregnant with profound significance the
more it is reflected upon.

XLIV. "For the union (*Henosis*) both of the First Father
(*Kronos*) and of the First of the Pure Gods is transcendent.
And because of this He is called 'Silent' by the Gods, and is

said to 'accord with Intellect (*Nous*)' and to become known
by souls through Intellect alone."—(*Proclus*)

When the Soul is elevated above itself in mystical contemplation by union with Intellect (*Spirit*) it becomes
identified with the Pure Thoughts or Words of God, where
nothing mortal can approach and no sound is to be heard,
for all processes or temporal activities are transcended,
and the Soul abides serene in its immaculate simplicity
before the Presence of the Silent One.

XLV. "For the Father (*Kronos*) perfected all things and
gave them over to the Second Intellect (*Zeus*), Whom ye,
all the race of mankind, call the First."

The Active Creator of the Cosmos is exoterically
regarded as the Absolute God or First Cause, but in the
Chaldean Mysteries He is the Second Mind, or Mind of
Mind. In the First Intellect all things pre-subsist intellectually as in the Mind of God; from Him they proceed and
are vivified through the Divine Intellectual Life; and, by
the Second Intellect, they are actually made manifest in
the worlds of form.

The Light of the Creative World is a divinely enkindled
Spiritual Sun.

XLVI. "Wherefore, by the Oracles also He is called the
'Father-begotten Light', because the unifying light shines
upon all.—(*Proclus*)

XLVII. "For utterly alone, gathering from the Father's
strength the Flower of Intellect, it hath power to know the
Intellect of the Father, to impart intellect to all the Fountains and Principles, and ever to whirl and abide in its
unwearied centre."

"Saturn, the First King of the Intellectual Gods, illuminates the pure and incorruptible nature of Intellect,
establishes His all-perfect power in His own summit of

intellectuals, abides in and at the same time proceeds from His Father."—(*Proclus in "Theol. of Plato"*)

"He leads forth the prolific power of Ideas and fills the Demiurgus with providential good."—(*ibid.*)

"He deifies the Intellectual Summit and illumines all things with Intelligible Light."—(*ibid.*)

"The Life-bearing Fountain of Souls is encompassed by Two Intellects."—(*Damascius*)

The Vivific Creative Fountain is called Rhea, of whom Proclus says: "This Goddess, being the middle of the Two Fathers—one of whom unifies, but the other differentiates intellectual multiplicity, and the one abides in himself, but the other produces and fabricates all things—She educes from Herself the demiurgic causes of wholes, but imparts Her own characteristic power to secondary natures in overflowing abundance—a power unifically comprehensive of the divisible rivers of life."—(*in "Theol. of Plato"*)

XLVIII. "Between the Fathers the Centre of Hecate is whirled."

The Vivific Intellectual Deity—Hecate, or Rhea —receives into Her bosom the Demiurgic power of the First Intellect and is said to pour this forth into the Second Intellect.

"She is the middle centre of the Paternal Intellectual Triad and the receiving bosom of Saturn, calling forth into the generation of wholes the causes which abide in Him, but unfolding this to all the Divine Powers; being filled from the Father prior to herself with intellectual and prolific power, but filling the Demiurgus and Father subsisting from Her with vivific abundance."—(*Proclus in "Theol. of Plato"*)

XLIX. "Fountain of all fountains, womb that holds all things together."

"This Goddess, binding together the sphere of the Intellectuals, and embosoming the vivific plenitude, · She emits all the intellectual powers in rivers of life."—(*ibid*)

"And the Source of Sources, and the bond of all sources."—(*Damascius*)

L. "And therefore the Third Intelligible Triad is the self-vital, about which the Oracles too say, that it is 'productive', 'the giver of life-bearing Fire', and that it fills the life-bearing bosom of Hecate and 'pours into the Synoches the prolific strength of the mightily potent Fire'."—(*Proclus*)

The vitalizing Fire of the Creative World has its unknown or occult origin in the Intelligible Paternal Profundity, whence it issues through the Synoches—the middle Archetypal Triad—and Hecate—the middle of the Intellectual Fathers.

"According to these three causes of the Vivific Goddess, which are co-arranged with the Demiurgus, the Cosmos is perfected by Him, according to the Fontal Crater, the Fountain of Excellencies, and the Original Efficient Cause of Nature." (*Proclus in "Theol. of Plato"*)

LI. "Concerning the life-bearing fountain of Rhea from which all life—divine, intellectual, of the soul, and that which is in the Cosmos—is engendered, the Oracles say: 'Rhea is the fount and river of the Blessed Intellectual Natures. For having first received the potentialities of all things in Her ineffable bosom, She poureth forth upon each perpetual generation.' "—(*Proclus*)

In the sacred mythoi, Jupiter (*Zeus*) is said to be the Son of Saturn (*Kronos*) and Rhea (*Cybele*), therefore, He is called "The Mind of Mind", for it is through Him that the Mind of the First Creative Father is made manifest.

LII. "For that Fire, which is First Beyond, shut not His

own Power in matter by actions, but by Mind. For the Mind of Mind is the Artificer of the Fiery Cosmos."

"Jupiter, being the Demiurgic Intellect, proceeds from another Intellect, superior, and being proximately established in union with this Divinity, from Him is made replete with integral intellectual good and is properly said to be the Son of Saturn."—(*Proclus on "Cratylus" of Plato*)

LIII. "For verily there was a Second Mass of Fire producing from itself all things, that the Cosmic Body might be perfectly unfolded, that the Cosmos might be plainly manifest and not appear membraneous."

The Demiurgus is a creator of wholes, that is, He makes the Cosmos manifest as one great integrality; all differentiation and particularization being the work of other powers.

"Jupiter is the cause of the unapparent life of the Cosmos, the supplier of Intellect, and the leader of intellectual perfection, but elevates all things to the Kingdom of Saturn.'—(*Proclus in "Theol. of Plato"*)

LIV. "By the bond of wondrous love, who first leapt forth from Intellect, clothing himself with the Fire with which He is bound, that He might mingle the ever-welling craters, pouring on to them the Flower of His own Fire."

The Creative Might of the Demiurgus is symbolized by the Thunderings of Jove, the All-creative Utterances or Root-words by which the manifested world is called into existence.

These Creative Sounds are the Triple Amiliktoi, the Inexorables, the Implacables, who give an unalterableness and an immutable purity to all the energies of the Primary Intellectual Triad—Saturn, Rhea, Jupiter.

"As Saturn, the first King of the Intellectual Gods, possesses a nature which does not verge to matter, through that pure monad or guard which is united to Him, namely the first of the Curetes; and as the Vivific Goddess Rhea possesses her stable and undeviating power from the second of the Guardian Deities; so also the Demiurgic Intellect possesses a guardian transcendency separate from others and a union withdrawing itself from multitude, through the third monad of the Curetes, who are the leaders of Purity."—*(Proclus on Parmenides)*

Thus, the Creator does not become identified with His creations, but produces them, mediately, through His Creative Words, which are the Curetes or Amiliktoi.

LV. "The Mind of the Father, borne on the impalpable rulers, who flash in their paths of inflexible relentless Fire."

The Thunderings or Creative Words of the Omnipotent Demiurgus are borne, as it were, on the wings of the Fiery Amiliktoi, who are themselves these very Creative Sounds which thrill through every realm of existence.

LVI. "For every Cosmos has inflexible intellectual sustainers."

They are the Curetes, the translucent Spotless Powers of the Fire-Self.

"Plato, following Orpheus, calls the inflexible and undefiled Triad of Intellectual Gods 'Curetic', meaning, that which is pure and incorruptible."—*(Proclus in "Theol. of Plato")*

"They preserve the whole progression of the Fathers undefiled, but supply them with inflexibility in their powers and immutability in their energies."—*(ibid.)*

"They are suspended from integral purity."

"The Three Undefiled Gods subsist with the Three Intellectual Fountains, are the guardians of the Fathers themselves, and are immutably and inflexibly established in them."—*(ibid.)*

LVII. "For from Him leap forth the Amiliktoi and the thunderings and the whirlwind-receiving vortices of the all-gleaming radiance of Father-begotton Hecate; and Hypezokus, Flower of the Fire, and the mighty breath beyond the fiery poles."

In a mystical sense the Empyrean Realm is surrounded by a Fiery Wall, which, as it were, separates the Seen from the Unseen, the Apparent from the Unapparent, the Manifested from the Unmanifested. This Fiery Wall is called Hypezokus or Oceanus, who is the Mysterious Boundary or Limit who separates the Above from the Below.

LVIII. "For just as a diaphragm (*Hypezokus*), and intellectual membrane, He separates."

Through Hypezokus, who terminates the Creative Septenary and is thus called the Flower of the Fire, that which is separated comes forth from that which is united, the partitive comes forth from the integral, the objective comes forth from the subjective.

LIX. "Thence leapeth forth the birth of all-various Hyle. Thence a fiery whirlwind rushing down dims the Flower of the Fire. For thence all things begin to extend their wondrous rays to the Below."

Thus, the Seven Powers of the One Integral Creative Fire are made manifest, and all things receive the seal of the Divine Prism, which originates in Kronos, the First Creative Father, and blossoms as a dazzling Flower of Fire in Oceanus.

Through Kronos, the Divine Creative Intellect is immanent in all souls.

Through Cybele, the Divine Creative Life is potential in all souls.

Through Zeus, the Demiurgic Intellect is to be made operative in all souls.

Through the Amiliktoi all souls are incorruptible and immortal, and destined to make manifest the Creative Powers of the Demiurgus.

And through Oceanus, the potentialities of all souls are to be made actual as they blossom into the Flower of the Creative Fire and pierce the Mystic Borders of Eternity, at the Pyramid of Creation and the Summit of Everlastingness.

'The Soul comes down into the world to act as a free servant, but only too often, it becomes an actual slave. If we yield to the seductions of matter, it is afterwards most difficult to get free from it. In this contest we require all our strength; we require the help of Heaven. This is the kind of contest which is related under the form of the story of the Labours of Hercules'.   *Synesius*

IV

The Ruling, Vivific, and Solar Principles

THE Empyrean Realm, according to the Chaldean Mystery Teaching, is threefold, comprising the Noetic World of the Paternal Profundity, the Noetic-noeric World of the Archetypal Ideas, and the Noeric World of the Sevenfold Creative Fires. Below the Empyrean, in an analogical sense, are the Realms of the Manifested Cosmos, which are also threefold, consisting of:

(1) The Hyperzonic World, in which are
   The Ruling Principles,
   The Vivific Principles, and
   The Solar Principles.
(2) The Azonic World, in which the Empyrean is objectively reflected in Nature as a whole.
(3) The Zonic World of precipitated Matter in which are
   The Inerratic Sphere,
   The 7 Planetary Spheres, and
   The Sublunary Sphere.

The Ruling, Vivific, and Solar Principles are hyperzonic, that is above all zones, as well as supercosmic, that is above the world of precipitated matter. They proceed immediately from the Creative Fires or Intellectual Fathers, and co-operate eternally with Them in fabricating, vivifying, and perfecting the whole of creation. They are the Divine Ruling Intelligences or Principles of all that is manifested or ever can be manifested.

"The Ruling Gods are collected into the Intellectual Order as into a summit, and subsist about it."—(*Proclus in "Theol. of Plato"*)

"Substanding Them (The Fathers) is the Ruling Principle of the immaterials."—(*Damascius*)

"They distribute the providence of the Demiurgus and Father; some arrange and adorn the universe with first, middle, and last forms of production; others educe the rivers of life and pour them on all things; and others elevate the natures that have proceeded and re-call them to the Father, presiding over purity and being the guardians of secondary natures."—(*Proclus in "Theol. of Plato"*)

A principle is an origin: it is that from which anything proceeds. Every conceivable thing in the universe can be traced to an immaterial principle, and all such principles bear some relation with the Ruling Principles which govern all that is generated in the great cosmos.

"Everything which is generated is generated from a principle, but the principle is not generated from anything."

"The Ruling Gods subsist by their very being."—(*ibid.*)

There is a distinction between generation and creation, which is analogous to that between the temporal and the eternal. Generated natures are born and exist in a perpetual condition of "becoming", whereas that which is created possesses permanent being and for ever "is", even although it may, metaphorically, pass into and out of the realms of generation.

"The Ruling Gods, who have the relation of Principles, are perfectly exempt from generated natures and are not co-arranged with them."

"They unfold monads into multitude, and collect multitude into unity."

"They also adapt wholes to parts, but comprehend parts in wholes."—(*ibid.*)

They are rulers of wholes and are unbegotten, presiding perpetually over all the spheres of existence, and all the wholenesses of the manifested universe.

"All the orders of the Principles or Rulers are suspended according to the nature of the Demiurgus and participate thence in an Intellectual energy."

"They conjoin all posterior natures to themselves and to those prior to themselves, and call forth the beneficent will of exempt causes into the providential care of secondary natures."—(*ibid.*)

Thus, the Ruling Principles subsist, as it were, between the unmanifested and the manifested, between the Creator, or Demiurgus, and the created, causing the one to be assimilated to the other.

LX. "The Principles, which comprehended intellectually the intelligible works of the Father, they clothed in sensible works and in bodies."

"Standing as bridges to communicate between the Father and Matter, fashioning that which is seen in the likeness of that which is unseen and writing the characters of the unseen on the worlds of visible form."—(*Damascius "De Princ.", II)

Every real principle has intimate relations with every other real principle; hence, through the Ruling Principles, which are also called "assimilative", there is a mysterious affinity, or sympathy between all things in the cosmos, and likewise, secondary natures may be assimilated or converted to primary natures.

"The Ruling Gods preside over the sympathy of things in the world and their communion with each other."

"The Assimilative Leaders of wholes produce and generate all things from themselves; for progressions are through similitude." "They convert all things to their principles, for every conversion is through similitude." —(*Proclus in "Theol. of Plato"*)

The Ruling Principles are threefold, and in the Orphic and Platonic Systems are known as: Jupiter, Neptune, and Pluto, the Sons of Saturn.

"The First establishes all things in the One Demiurgus, from Whom they proceed: the Second unfolds all things into progression; and the Third converts all things to itself."

"The First adorns the inerratic sphere and the circulations of it; the Second governs the planetary region and perfects the multiform, efficacious, and prolific motions in it; and the Last administers the sublunary region and intellectually perfects the terrestrial world."—(*ibid.*)

"According to every division of the universe, the summits are Jovian, the middles belong to Neptune, and the extremities to Pluto."

"Jupiter has the relation of a Father; Neptune receives Souls descending into generation; but Pluto frees Souls from generation."

"The whole period of life has a triple division: that which is prior to generation is Jovian; that which is in or of generation is Neptunian; and that which is posterior to generation is Plutonian."—(*Scholia of Proclus on "Cratylus" of Plato*)

THE VIVIFIC PRINCIPLES

The triad of Vivific Principles in the Chaldean System has a correspondence with the Coric Triad of the Orphic Theogony.

(1) Hecate is the same as Coric Diana, the Gateway of Life.
(2) Ruling Soul is the same as Coric Proserpine, the Queen of the Soul in Generation.
(3) Ruling Virtue is the same as Coric Minerva, the Fount of Virtue.

"There are three Vivific Monads—Diana, Proserpine, Minerva—and the first of these is the summit of the Triad, who converts to herself the Third; but the Second is a power vivific of wholes: and the Third is a divine and undefiled intellect, comprehending in one, in a ruling manner, total virtues."—(*Proclus on "Theol. of Plato"*)

"The dominion of Hecate is established as an hyparxis or summit of this Triple Vivific Order; Ruling Soul is that of a middle power, which is generative of wholes; and Ruling Virtue is according to an intellectual conversion."—(*Scholia of Proclus on "Cratylus" of Plato*)

Hecate or Diana is the Gateway of Life, the Vivific Ruling Principle Who is said to be filled with undefiled powers from the Amiliktoi, and to impart this characteristic to all beings that pass through Her mysterious gateway, at the crossroads of life and death. For death is but an entrance into Life Supernal: and life is but a birth into the realms of generation.

Coric Proserpine, the Ruling Soul, is the power whereby the Soul preserves the middle or abiding subsistence at the same time that it verges upward or downward, either to the Above or the Below. Hence, when the Soul is identified with the realms of nature and matter, Proserpine is said to be united to Pluto; but in her pre-existent and post-existent states, when reigning on high purified from hyle or matter, Proserpine is said to be united with Jupiter.

Coric Minerva, or Ruling Virtue, reveals the way of return, converts ends to beginnings, "preserves the order of wholes undefiled and unvanquished by matter, and fills all who are able to participate with intellectual light"—(*ibid.*)

She is evidently referred to in the following fragment of the Oracles:

LXI. "There appeared in it both Virtue and Wisdom and all-mindful Justice."

Proclus says: "The Oracles, too, speak of this light when, in expounding the nature of the animation with which the Fountain of Souls animates all things, they say:

LXII. "From about the hollows beneath the ribs of Her right side (Hecate's) there bursts in mighty fullness a fountain of Primordial Soul, animating to the uttermost light, fire, ether, worlds."

LXIII. "In the left side of Hecate there is a Fountain of Virtue, remaining wholly within, not sending forth its virginity."

LXIV. "And about the shoulders of the Goddess, vast Nature hangs."

Thus do the Oracles, in profound allegorical language, describe the Great World Mother, Whose incarnation in the realms of manifestation causes all things to be ensouled and to participate in the plenitude of providential life which thrills through the whole of creation.

LXV. "In accordance with the Purpose of the Father, I, the Soul, dwell, animating all things with heat."

THE SOLAR PRINCIPLES

Since all the Principles are hyperzonic, they are above and beyond all zones and are not limited to or confined by space in its literal sense. All the suns of the spatial and visible universe proceed from and depend upon the Hyperzonic and Invisible Solar Principles, which are to the suns what the suns are to the lesser orbs which proceed from and depend upon them.

"The Demiurgus, possessing and comprehending in Himself the Solar Fountain, generates likewise, in conjunction with the Principles and Rulers, the Solar Powers

and the Triad of Solar Gods, through Whom all things are elevated, perfected, and filled with Intellectual Goods."
—*(Proclus in "Theol. of Plato")*

The Solar Powers are also called "The Triple Sun", which is invisible and intellectual, within and beyond all the suns of the universe.

In the Orphic System the Triple Sun is:

(1) Mercury, who is the Super-essential Light.
(2) Venus-Urania, who is the Intelligible Light, and
(3) Apollo, who is the Sovereign Sun.

"The First is enunciative of Truth and the Intellectual Light which subsists occultly in the Gods Themselves; The Second is subversive of everything confused and exterminative of all disorder; and the Third renders all things commensurable and friendly to each other, through harmonic reasons."—*(ibid.)*

The Triple Sun is the Light of the Divine Nous or Intellect, which is hidden, as it were, in the heart of the Great World Mother as well as in the deeps of the Soul.

Mercury reveals the Light of Divine Truth; Venus-Urania reveals the Light of Divine Beauty; and Apollo reveals the Light of Divine Goodness or Harmony.

Although this Triple Sun is a dazzling light in itself, it is surrounded by a profound mystical darkness.

> Beyond the darkness, starry-eye'd, profound,
> The stable roots, deep-fix'd by Thee, are found.
> —*(Orphic Hymn to Apollo)*

The starry-eyed darkness, beyond which Apollo is said to fix his roots, is the sphere above the fixed stars.

"The Orb of the Sun revolves in the starless sphere, far above the height of the inerratic sphere, hence it does not hold the middle place among the planetery spheres, but of the three worlds."—(*Emp. Julian in Orat.*)

Apollo, as the Sovereign Sun, is the Solar Logos. He is in the Hyperzonic World what Jupiter, the Demiurgus, is in the Creative or Noeric World, for as the latter illuminates the supermundane order with Intellectual Light, so the former illuminates all zonic orders with Hyperzonic Light.

Thus, beyond Apollo is the Light or Fire of Jupiter, and beyond Jupiter is the Paternal Profundity and the Infinite ONE; therefore the "stable roots" of Apollo are fixed ultimately in the ONE but have their extensions in all realms, like the branches of the macrocosmic tree.

"As trees by their roots are firmly established in the earth and all that pertains to them is through this earthly; after the same manner, Divine Natures are by their Summits rooted in the ONE, and each of them is a unity and one, through an unconfused union with the ONE."—(*Proclus, Comments on "Parmenides"*)

The visible sun, which is the outermost expression of the Triple Sun of the Solar Principles, is therefore a most appropriate emblem of Deity, for it repeats, in terms of itself, all the principles that precede it.

As the Oracles declare, the Sun is:

LXVI. "A Fire, a Channel of Fire, and a Dispenser of Fire."

And through this, all things participate in the Solar Fire, with its light, heat, and force, as well as all the mystical analogies of these three qualities.

Thus, when identified with the Powers of the Ruling Principles, the Soul is able to work eternal works even in the realms of time and space.

LXVII. "Performing, when the channels are mingled, works of imperishable fire."

"Bringing into sameness, according to a certain ineffable union, that which fills and that which is filled, and, on the one hand, disposing it, free from matter and in proportion to its light, to the illumination, and, on the other, calling it forth to the sharing of the Light."—(*Proclus on "Republic"*)

"According to this discourse, the Sun also being supermundane, sends forth the Fountains of Light, and the most mystical of the discourses hand down the conception that the wholeness of Him is that which subsists in the Supermundane Orders; for there is 'the true Solar World' and the 'Totality of Light', as the Chaldean Oracles declare."—(*Proclus on "Timaeus"*)

When the Soul is united consciously with this Spiritual Sun then it is at one with the Integral Divine Light from which nothing is hidden, either on earth or in heaven.

'As soon, therefore, as the soul gravitates towards body in this first production of herself, she begins to experience a material tumult, that is matter flowing into her essence. And this is what Plato remarks in the Phaedo, that the soul is drawn into body staggering with recent intoxication, signifying by this, the new drink of matter's impetuous flood. Hence oblivion, the companion of intoxication, begins silently to creep into the recesses of the soul.

For if souls retained in their descent to bodies the memory of divine concerns, of which they were conscious in the heavens, there would be no dissension among men about Divinity. But all, indeed, in descending, drink of oblivion; though some more, and others less. On this account though truth is not apparent to all men on the earth, yet all exercise their opinions about it, because a defect of memory is the origin of opinion. But those discover most who have drunk least of oblivion, because they easily remember what they had known before in the heavens.'

Macrobius

V

Nature and Matter

The World-view afforded by the Chaldean Oracles is integral in the real sense, for it embraces the innermost and uppermost principles of the Empyrean and Subjective Cosmos, as well as the objective realm of Nature and precipitated Matter, which are the outermost and nethermost expressions of all the higher, spiritual, and noetic principles.

Viewed from below upwards and outwards, the manifested Cosmos consists of the Sublunary Sphere, the Seven Planetary Spheres, and the Inerratic Sphere or Sphere of Fixed Stars, while above and beyond and pervading all these is the Ethereal Realm with its sub-divisions.

Psellus, in his Exposition of the Oracles, says:

"There are seven worlds of form, one empyrean and the first, after this three ethereal, and then three material worlds, namely, the inerratic sphere, the seven planetary spheres, and the sublunary region. They also assert that there are two solar worlds, one which is subservient to the ethereal profundity, and the other, zonic, being one of the seven spheres."

All that exists is the result of the union of Form and Matter; the form is, as it were, reflected from the Archetypal World into the Azonic and Ethereal Realm of Nature as a whole, while the matter, which in its totality is called "Hyle", is composed of the various elements arising out of the chaos or void when impregnated by the higher principles which proceed into manifestation from the Creative Fire of the Demiurgus or Divine Creative Mind.

"That which comes into being must be in bodily form and seen and divided, and deprived of fire nothing would ever be seen." (*Proclus in "Timaeus"*)

LXVIII. "It is indeed an imitation of Mind (Nous), but that which is brought forth has something of body."

"The Demiurgus Himself, by antecedently comprehending Nature, governs the universe."—(*ibid.*)

In the Timaeus Plato unfolds in mystical and allegorical language the manner in which Jupiter, or the Demiurgus directs the Mundane Gods to the Work of generating mortal natures and animals, in completion of His own creations, which necessarily partake of His own immortal nature.

"Gods of Gods, of Whom I am the Demiurgus and Father, whatever is produced by Me is indissoluble, such being My Will in its fabrication.

Three genera of mortals yet remain to be produced: without the generation of these the universe would be imperfect, for it would not contain every kind of animated being in its spacious extent.

That mortal natures may exist, therefore, and that the Cosmos may be truly integral, convert yourselves according to your natures to the fabrication of animated creatures, and whatever among these is of such a nature as to deserve the title of immortal, which is called divine, obtains sovereignty in them and willingly pursues justice and reverences you—of this I myself will deliver the seed and beginning. It is your work to accomplish the rest, to weave together the mortal and immortal natures, by this means fabricating and generating animated beings, causing them to increase by supplying them with nutriment and receiving them back again when dissolved by corruption. . ."

"At the same time, He Who orderly disposed all these things, remained, as befitting Him, in His own nature, and His Children heard and were obedient to their Father's Word, and receiving from Him the immortal principle of mortal creatures, in imitation of their own creation, they borrowed portions of fire and earth and water from the world, which were thereafter to be returned, these they took and welded together."—*(Plato in "Timaeus")*

"These fashion that which is indivisible and sensible and things with bodily form, and those which are co-arranged with Matter."—*(Damascius, de Princ)*

"Since the Gods spake these things to Theurgists; for although They are without body, for your sakes They put on bodies in the autoptic visions, since you cannot participate in incorporeal natures incorporeally because of the corporeal nature in which you are centred."—*(Proclus on "Republic")*

"For it says that this (the light) is that which first received the everlasting allotments of the Gods and makes manifest in itself the autoptic visions, for in this the Oracle says:

LXIX. "That which is formless is given form."—*(Simplicius in Phys.)*

This refers to the manner in which the noetic and noumenal ideas of the Archetypal Realm are reflected and expressed by the Gods in the realms of form and matter. These reflected types, in their totality, are comprehended by Nature, who, according to the Oracles, is the Divine Ruling Principle of the sensible world.

LXX. "For unwearied Nature ruleth over worlds and works, that the whirling heaven may run its everlasting course and the swift Sun may come about his centre in his accustomed way."

Proclus says: "From the Timaeus it appears that Plato does not consider either matter or material form or body or natural powers as worthy to be called Nature, though it has been thus denominated by others. Nor does he think proper to call Nature 'Soul'; but, establishing its essence between Soul and corporeal powers, he considers it as inferior to the former through its being divided about bodies and its incapacity of conversion to itself, but as surpassing the latter through containing the productive principles, and by generating and vivifying every part of the visible world. For Nature verges towards bodies, and is inseparable from their fluctuating empire; but Soul is separate from body, is established in herself, and subsists both from herself and another; from another, that is Intellect (Nous) through participation, and from herself, on account of not verging to body, but abiding in her own essence and at the same time illuminating the obscure nature of matter with a secondary life."

"Nature, therefore, is the last of the causes which fabricate the corporeal and sensible world, bounds the progressions of incorporeal essences, and is full of reasons and powers through which she governs mundane affairs."

"Nature proceeds from the Vivific Goddess Rhea, for as the Oracle says: 'And about the shoulders of the Goddess, vast Nature hangs' (LXIV) from Whom all life is derived, both that which is intellectual and that which is inseparable from the objects of its government. But Nature, being thus suspended, She pervades and inspires all things without impediment. Hence, the most inanimate of things participate of a certain soul, and corruptible natures remain perpetually in the world, being connected and comprehended by the causes of forms which Nature contains."—*(Proclus in "Theol of Plato")*

In the Oracles the Moon is identified with Nature as the ultimate expression of the Ruling Vivific Principles of the

Hyperzonic Realm, just as the Sun is of the Ruling Solar Principles.

"The Divinity (the Moon) has the relation of Nature and of a Mother with respect to generation or the sublunary region; for all things are convolved and co-increased by her when she increases, but are diminished when she diminishes. This Goddess, too, benevolently leads into light the unapparent productive principles of Nature."
—*(Proclus on "Timaeus")*

In passing from the unapparent or unmanifested to the apparent and hylic realm all things proceed out of the womb of the ethereal profundity, through the power of the Sun, and become precipitated in the Sublunary sphere through the influence of the Moon.

LXXI. "The centres of the hylic world are fixed in the ether about it."

LXXII. "It (the world) is a part of ether, of the Sun, of the rivers of the Moon, and of the air."
Proclus in Timaeus says that the Oracles "everywhere arrange the moon after the sun and the air after the moon, both when they deliver the order of them from above and when from below", as the following fragments evince.

LXXIII. "O Ether, Sun, breath of the Moon, and Ye Rulers of the Air; of the solar circles, the ringing dances of the Moon, and the airy depths."

LXXIV. "And the etherial course, the measureless rush of the Moon, and the aerial streams."

LXXV. "The wide air, the lunar course, and the everlasting pole of the Sun."

LXXVI. "And the lunar course and the procession of the stars."

"He (The Demiurgus) fixed also a great multitude of inerratic stars, not by laborious and painful effort, but with a stability that could admit of no wandering. He compelled the Fire to the Fire."—*(Proclus in "Timaeus")*

LXXVII. The Demiurgus is said to make the whole world "from fire and water and earth and all-nourishing ether".

This fire of the Demiurgus is not the same as the terrestrial or sublunary fire, but is rather a celestial wholeness of fire from which the fire of the visible Sun itself springs.

"For the life-engendering channel proceeds as far as the centre, as the Oracles say, speaking of the midmost of the five centres extending from above right through the centre of the earth to the opposite extreme."—*(Proclus in "Timaeus")*

LXXVIII. "And fifth, in the midst, another fiery way whence the life-bearing fire descends even to the hylic channels."

The "five centres" are, no doubt, the five planets, which, with the Sun and the Earth, make up the seven mystical planets of the Chaldean mysteries.

"The Demiurgus suspended six zones, and for the seventh hurled into the midst the fire of the Sun."—*(Emp. Julian)*

LXXIX. The Oracles define a centre as that "From which all lines (or rays) to the periphery are equal."

LXXX. "For the Father caused to swell forth seven firmaments of worlds, confining the heaven in a curved form."

These seven firmaments of worlds are also called "cosmocrators", each of which is said to have its appropriate archontic and angelic principles.

Thomas Taylor, in his "Theoretic Arithmetic", quoting an anonymous writer, says: The Ancients "very properly call the starry orbs 'herds'; either in so far as they alone among corporeal masses revolve perfectly about the centre, or because the Oracles in their discourses on Nature lay down that they hold the position of 'binders' or 'uniters' which in the same manner they call 'herds' (ἀγέας = *agelas*) and by the insertion of the gamma 'angles' (ἀγγέλος). Wherefore the stars which rule over each of these herds they call daemons like angels, and archangels—and these are seven in number."

Nature, as well as the Divine and Celestial Principles, operates through the media of angels and daemons. There are innumerable hosts of these Lesser Powers, which govern all the operations of the various Kingdoms of Nature. In the Oracles, the Daemons are symbolically called "Dogs", because of their watchful and guardian characteristics.

LXXXI. "She (Nature) is the Charioteer of the airy, terrestrial, and watery dogs."

LXXXII. "Nature persuades us that the Daemons are pure and that even the growths of evil matter are useful and good."

That is to say, the beneficent operations of the angelic hosts turn all things to good and useful ends.

LXXXIII. "Out of the womb of earth leap Dogs terrestrial that unto mortal never show true sign."

There are watery powers as well as powers of earth and fire.

The watery, in reference to divine concerns, signifies the providential characteristic of water which is analogous to the undivided sovereignty of the Gods, "Wherefore the Oracles call these Gods Water-walkers".—*(Proclus in "Timaeus")*

LXXXIV. "The nymphs of the fountains and all the water spirits and the depths of the earth and the air and the gleaming hollows are the lunar riders and the rulers of matter, celestial, starry, and that which is of the abysses."

Thus is the great Chaldean world-view completed, beginning from the Ineffable Paternal Profundity of the Most High, and passing through a sublime and wondrous Hierarchy of Divine, Celestial, and Angelic principles, ruling over all the realms and planes of existence in the macrocosm, from the first to the very last of things, even to the darkest and most gross aspect of Matter, in which, as the Oracles say, is the "light-hating place".

LXXXV. "All Nature in generation, in which are the 'turbid bulk of Matter', and the 'Light-hating World', as the Gods say, and the 'winding streams by which many are drawn under'."

"There are three hylic worlds of which the last is called terrestrial and light-hating, which is the place below the Moon, having Matter in itself also, which they call the Abyss."—*(Psellus)*

LXXXVI. "Alas, alas, for these (those in the 'light-hating world') the Earth maketh lamentation even unto their children."

For the Soul, merged in Matter, is indeed in a hylic prison house, seeking ever the Realms of Light of its True Home. The Way of Return is the Great Ascent, which the Oracles unfold in a most luminous and inspiring manner.

VI

The Descent of the Soul

"VERILY those Souls, by far most blest of all, are poured forth to Earth from Heaven. Most blissful they and ineffable their fate, who from thy Shining Self, O King, yea, and from Zeus Himself, are born, under the compelling might of Destiny."—(LXXXVII)

The human soul is a child of Divine Parents, according to the Oracles; it is not born of the earth, nor is it evolved by Nature, nor generated by human parents, nor is it a mere offspring of Chance or of purposeless mechanical or instinctual processes.

In its essential nature the Soul bears an intimate relation and similitude with that which is Divine, and howsoever far it may seem to journey into darkness and oblivion, it for ever retains in its inmost deeps the seal and memory—howsoever dim—of its divine origin.

It is essentially immortal, although it puts on, as it were, a mortal and corruptible vesture in its descent into generation. But in itself it is distinct from the corporeal and natural body which is generated in conjunction with human parents and Nature. Through the instrumentality of these, the Soul is born in a physical body, which is derived from Earth, but the Soul itself comes from Heaven.

The heavenly part of man is spiritual and is called Intellect or Nous in the Oracles; this is blended with the corporeal part which the Soul puts on in its descent, and thus man is a spiritual-corporeal being, with a supernatural destiny as well as a natural heritage or fate.

LXXXVIII. "Binding Mind (*Nous*) in Soul, and Soul in dull Body, the Father of Gods and men established them therein."

LXXXIX. "These things the Father conceived, and man became a living Soul."

"Placing Intellect in Soul, but Soul in body, He (The Demiurgus) fabricated the all."—*(Plato in "Timaeus")*

"The Demiurgus (or Zeus) produces all things simultaneously and eternally; for by His very being, and according to an eternal intelligence of wholes, He generates from Himself supermundane and mundane beings, intellects, souls, natures, bodies, and matter itself."—*(Proclus on "Timaeus")*

"Placing Soul in the middle, He (Demiurgus) extended it through the whole of the world."—*(Plato in "Timaeus")*

"But the Soul, unfolding herself to the extremity of the universe, from the middle, circularly covered it as with a veil, herself being convolved in herself."—*(ibid.)*

The Soul is a tri-unity; it possesses an essence peculiar to itself; a power or potentiality characteristic of the principles which are above itself; and an energy or activity through which it unfolds its latent capacity and becomes identified with that which is below as well as above itself. These three—essence, power, energy—are united in the Soul, as Proclus says, and make it what it is.

"Having mingled these two with essence and made one thing of the three, He again divided this whole into appropriate parts."—*(Proclus on "Timaeus")*

XC. "Blending the spark of the Soul with two concordant unities, Mind and Divine Breath, to these He added a Third, Pure Love, Who bindeth all things in holy bonds and is master of all."

The blending of these three unities in the Soul give to it, throughout all its peregrinations, an unquenchable thirst for beauty, an ineradicable tendency towards goodness, and an inextinguishable yearning for truth.

XCI. "With deep love" filling the Soul.

XCII. "The Father leapeth not (into the Soul) with fear, but infuseth persuasion."

"The Paternal Mind (Nous) hath sown Symbols in Souls."—*(Psellus)*

"Love is neither to be placed in the first, nor among the last of beings. Not in the first, because the object of love is superior to love; nor among the last, because the lover participates of love."

"Love, therefore, must be established between the object of love and the lover—it is posterior to the Beautiful, but prior to every nature endued with love."

"There are Three Hypostases in the Intelligible Gods: the first is characterized by the Good and comprehends the Good Itself, abiding for ever where, according to the Oracles, the Paternal Monad abides; the second is characterized by Wisdom and abides where the First Intelligence flourishes; and the third is characterized by Beauty and abides with the most beautiful of the Intelligibles."

"These three subsist unically and causally in the Intelligibles, but unfold themselves into light in the ineffable Order of the Gods as 'Faith, Truth, and Love'."—(XCIII)

"Faith establishes all things in the Good, Truth unfolds all the Knowledge in beings, and Love converts all things and assimilates them into the nature of the Beautiful."

"Love, therefore, supernally descends from the Intelligibles into mundane natures, calling all things upward to Divine Beauty. Truth proceeds through all things, illuminating them all with Knowledge; and Faith proceeds through the universe, establishing all things unically in the Good."

"Hence, as the Oracles assert, 'all things are governed

by, and abide in, these three', and on this account they exhort mystics to conjoin themselves with Divinity through this triad."—*(Proclus in "Theol. of Plato")*

"There are three lives of the Soul, of which the best and most perfect is that according to which it is conjoined with the Gods and lives a life most allied to theirs, and through the highest similitude is united to them, not subsisting merely from itself, but from them, energizing according to its own Intellect, inspired by the ineffable idea of the ONE which it contains, and, connecting like with like, its own light with the Light of the Gods, and that which is most unitive in its own essence and life, with the ONE, Who is above all essence and life.

"The second life to this in dignity and power has a middle allotment in the centre of the Soul, according to which it is converted to itself, descending from a divinely inspired life, and, identified with Intellect and Knowledge as the principles of its energy, it unfolds the multitude of its innate reasons, surveys the all-various mutations of forms, unites the objects of intellect with intellect itself, and expresses its conceptions in an intellectual and intelligible mode.

"The third life of the Soul is that which accords with its secondary powers, and energizes together with them, employing phantasy and irrational faculties, and is immersed in things of a subordinate nature."—*(Proclus on "Republic")*

"The descent of the Soul into body separates it from divine Souls, from whom it is filled with intelligence, power, and purity, and conjoins it with generation and nature and material things, from which it partakes of oblivion, aberration, and ignorance. For, in its descent, multiform activities and various vestments become associated with it, which draw it down into a mortal composition and darken its vision of Real Being."—*(Proclus on "First Alcibiades")*

But in the very core of its essence, the Soul for ever preserves a spark of the all-nourishing Fire of Almighty Zeus, which as it were the Soul, like Prometheus, plucks from the Divine Fire as it descends from on High.

Wherefore, as Proclus says, "comprehending intellectually the works of the Father—

"XCIV. They escape the reckless wing of allotted fate; they abide in God, drawing to themselves the topmost glory of the flaming Beacons streaming down in light from the Father. From these, as they descend, the Soul plucketh of their empyrean fruits the Soul-nourishing flower."

The nature of the Soul is such that it escapes precise definition and can only be expressed by analogy and paradox. Although it is said to be placed in body, yet since, mystically, it unfolds itself to the extremity of the universe, it comprehends all space and therefore, in this sense, the body is in the Soul.

According to fragments of the Oracles, the Soul is—

XCV. "A part of the Divine Fire", and a "gleaming fire", and "a thought of the Father", and therefore, her form is immaterial and self-subsistent.—*(Psellus)*

In her descent into generation, from the Empyrean realm, the Soul may be conceived as collecting the essences or elements of the bodies or vehicles through which she is to manifest herself, as Proclus, quoting the Oracles, says: she "collects" the body, taking "a part of the Sun and the Moon and that which is contained in the air".

She does, indeed, pass through the ethereal worlds, the inerratic sphere or sphere of fixed stars, and the seven planetary spheres, before she is born of the sublunary region with a physical body. Thus man, in terms of himself, is an epitome of the great universe.

"Man is a microcosm; for he has Intellect and reason, an immortal and a mortal body, and a nature that is differentiated in an analogous manner to that of the universe. Hence also, as some are accustomed to say, his intellectual principle is analogous to the sphere of the fixed stars, but his reason, which is theoretic, is analogous to the planet Saturn, while his ordinative and political part is compared to Jupiter, his irrational and irascible nature to Mars, his power of expression and speech to Mercury, that which is epithumetic to Venus, that which is sensitive to the Sun, and that which is vegetative to the Moon. The luciform vehicle is analogous to the heavens, but the mortal body to the sublunary region."—*(Proclus on "Timaeus")*

The Soul is the mysterious unity by which the manifold and diverse parts of man's nature are harmonized and blended into a single human being, and because he is a miniature of the macrocosm, in knowing himself he comes to know all that the universe stands for.

XCVI. "O Man, bold nature's handiwork."

"The Soul, by verging to a material life, kindles, indeed, a light in the body, but becomes herself involved in darkness."—*(Proclus on "Theol. of Plato")*

"The corporeal-formed life which proceeds from the Soul and has the relation of splendour to it, is said by Plato to be divisible about bodies. For Intellect, indeed, is analogous to the Sun, Soul to the light proceeding from the Sun, and the partible life to the splendour of the light."—*(Proclus on "Timaeus")*

XCVII. "From every side extend reins of fire to the unformed Soul."

"For together with the Intellectual Light of the Father she calls into existence the works of Nature. For it is the Soul which hath adorned the vast heaven and adorneth it with the Father's aid. But her head is established on high."—*(Proclus in "Timaeus")*

XCVIII. For the Soul being "by the Power of the Father a radiant fire both remains immortal and is mistress of life, and hath power to fill with plenitude the many wombs of the cosmos".

Whilst Souls dwell on high in union with the Father they live a supernal life according to Divine Providence and transcend the limitations imposed by the laws of Fate; but when they descend into manifestation, although these laws are announced to them by the Demiurgus, as Plato says, yet they drink of the waters of Lethe or forgetfulness, and lose temporarily the memory of their pristine purity and bliss.

"When Souls become mundane, then also they survey the power and dominion of Fate, supernally suspended from Providence, and receive the Laws of Destiny. For the Demiurgus revealed Nature to them, as something different from themselves, but He announced to them the laws of Fate, as innate in them."—*(Proclus on "Timaeus")*

"But the Oracles celebrate in a particular manner the Fountain of all empyrean Soul, that is, the empyrean, etherial and hylic; and they distinguish this Fountain from the whole Vivific Goddess, from whom they suspend also the whole of Fate, and indicate two processions or orders, the one that of Soul, but the other that which we call Fatal, that it is, the order of Fate or Fortune. And they derive the Soul from the former, but say that it is sometimes subject to Fate when it becomes irrational and changes its lord, serving Fate instead of Providence."—*(Proclus on Providence)*

"Fate is comprehensive of all the mundane laws, which the Demiurgus reveals to Souls, that they may, through Him, ultimately be led to a knowledge of universal wholeness and be enabled to choose that which is adapted to them in their particular elections of different lives and activities.

"A selfish life tends to darkness and negation, but a

pious life leads the Soul to the celestial realms and is characterized by universality. Each of the lives of the Soul is according to the laws of Fate, but Souls lead themselves, as Plotinus says, whither the law, which is within them, announces. For this is the peculiarity of the Providence of the Gods, to conduct inwardly the objects for which it provides.

"Nature, also, inserting material and corporeal and formal powers in bodies, moves them according to these powers; in a much greater degree, therefore, do the Gods move Souls through the powers which they disseminate in them. Hence, if they lead Souls according to the laws of Fate, these laws, also, are innate in Souls.

"And they presubsist intellectually in the Demiurgus, for the Divine Law is established with Him. But they are inherent in perfected Souls and according to them they govern the world; and they conduct themselves to their allotted places, themselves moving themselves; and through deliberate choice they act erroneously or with rectitude; but through the law they produce for themselves an order of life in conformity with the effects of their actions."—*(Proclus on "Theol. of Plato")*

"The rational and intellectual Soul, in whatever way it may energize, is superior to body and sense, and in itself is essentially independent of these; hence, when it energizes according to its own nature it transcends the influence of Fate, but when it falls into sense and becomes identified with that which is irrational and corporeal, it follows the natures that are inferior to itself, and, living with them as with intoxicated neighbours, is held in subjection by a cause that has dominion over things that are contrary to the rational essence."

"Not only Plato, but likewise the Oracles have revealed these things to us; for in the first place they ordered those men who were thought worthy to be the auditors of those mystic discourses to—

"XCIX. 'Look not upon Nature, for her name is Fate.' They also order them to—

"C. 'Increase not thy Fate, of which there is no end.'
"And, again, they exhort them to turn from the life which is according to Fate.

"CI. 'For theurgists fall not among the fate-driven herd,' by all which they withdraw us from the senses and the corporeal desires, for through these we become corporeal and are then acted upon from necessity by Fate."—*(Proclus on Providence and Fate)*

CII. "According to the Oracles the multitude of men 'who go in a herd' is to be avoided."—*(Proclus in "Alcibiades")*
By the "herd", the Oracles signify the multitude of unawakened and unregenerated human beings who are contented to follow a life according to the dictates of natural instincts and impulses and who, as Proclus says, become identified with inferior natures as with intoxicated neighbours.

CIII. "Do ye not know that God is wholly good? O ye impatient of toil, be sober."

CIV. "But man, since he hath an intelligible principle, must bridle his Soul that she may verge not to the unhappy earth but find salvation."

CV. "Lest being plunged in the frenzies of earth and the compelling necessities of Nature" its life should be destroyed.
The consequences of the Soul's fall from the intrinsic dignity of its true self is that man becomes the slave of his lower nature, which holds him as in a prison, wherein he

experiences the scourges of the Furies, as well as the bondage of the Fates.

CVI. "The Furies are the throttlers of men."

"As Psellus explains, the powers that punish guilty souls bind them to their material passions, and in these, as it were, suffocate them; such punishment being finally the means of purification, nor do these powers only afflict the vicious, but even such as convert themselves to an immaterial essence; for these, through their connection with matter require a purification of this kind."—*(Thomas Taylor in Orphic Hymns)*

But howsoever low the Soul may fall from its real estate, it can never become the Soul of a sub-human creature. As Proclus says: "that the passing into irrational beings is contrary to the nature of Souls, the Oracles teach us when they declare that—

"CVII. 'This a law from the Blessed Ones that naught can break' and that the human Soul 'completes its life again in men and not in beasts'."

"But the transmigrations of Souls, if they take place into such as are rational, then they become the Souls of particular bodies; if into such as are irrational, then they follow these *externally* in the same manner as our presiding daemons attend us in their beneficent operations; for the rational part never becomes the Soul of an irrational nature. But the truth of transmigration is evinced by the circumstances which are associated with the birth of individuals; for why are some born blind, others imbecile, and others with a vicious temperament? Moreover, since Souls are essentially adapted to function according to their peculiar purposes in bodies, it is not proper that when they have once deserted them they should remain indolent for ever; for if Souls did not return again into bodies, it is necessary that either they should be infinite in number, or that others should continually be produced by divinity. But there can be nothing actually infinite in the world, for that which is infinite can never exist in that which is finite. But neither is it possible that others can be produced, for everything in which something new may be generated is necessarily imperfect, but it is requisite that the world should be perfect, because it is produced from a Perfect Source."—(*Sallust on The Gods and the World*)

Therefore, although man cannot himself descend to the animal kingdom, yet he can become so closely identified therewith that the light of heaven seems almost quenched.

CVIII. "Thy vessel the beasts of the earth shall inhabit."

CIX. "Hard to turn, with burden on back, without share in the light."
For those who lead an evil life:

CX. "They are no great way off from dogs irrational."
In the light of such disasters that may befall the erring Soul, the exhortations of the Oracles are pregnant with significance.

CXI. "Stoop not down, for a precipice lieth beneath, sheer from the earth, drawing down by a descent of seven steps, neath which is the Throne of dire Necessity."
The seven steps are the seven subterranean hells which are the antitheses of the seven celestial spheres.

CXII. "Nor stoop down to the darkly-gleaming world, beneath which is ever spread an abyss, formless and obscure, wrapped in befouling gloom, joying in shadows, where the Intelligible hath no place; precipitous and winding, a blind depth, ever turning, in perpetual embrace with an unseen body, inert and lifeless."

CXIII. "Store not in thy mind the earth's vast measurements, for the Tree of Truth groweth not upon earth; nor assemble thy calculations to measure the measures of the Sun; not for thy sake doth he run his course, but by the Eternal Will of the Father. Let go the rush of the moon; for she circleth ever by the operation of Necessity. Not for thy sake was the starry procession brought forth. Never true is the wide flight of birds through the high air, nor the dissections of sacrificial entrails: all these are toys, the support of mercenary fraud. Flee thou from such, if to the Holy Paradise of True Piety thou wouldest enter in, where Virtue, Wisdom, and Good Law together dwell."

Every species of divination is necessarily qualified by the limitations of time and space, but the Soul's victory over temporal and spatial conditions depends upon its introduction or initiation into that which is eternally and immutably established above all that belongs to time and space and motion. Hence, the Way of Return is to be found first within the deeps of the Soul where the seal or word of divinity is concealed, and by the interpretation of which the Soul enkindles the light of divine ideas which makes plain the pathway of the Great Ascent.

CXIV. "But the Mind of the Father receiveth not her (the Soul's) will until she cometh out of oblivion and speaketh the Word, restoring to herself the memory of the Holy Covenant of the Father."

'The Abyss of God calleth to the abyss in us.'   *Ruysbroeck.*

VII

The Ascent of the Soul

"LET the immortal depth of thy Soul lead thee, and open all thine eyes earnestly to the Above."—(CXV).

This exhortation, like the voice of the Blessed Ones of the forgotten past reverberating through all the ages, is the Call to all true Aspirants to make ready for the Great Ascent of the Soul of the Sacred Mountain.

"Socrates, in the Alcibiades, rightly observes that the Soul, retiring into herself, will behold all other things and deity itself. For, verging to her own unity and to the centre of all life, laying aside multitude and the variety of all the manifold powers which she contains, she ascends to the highest watch-tower of real beings. For the Soul, when looking to things posterior to herself, beholds only the shadows and images of beings; but when she turns to herself, she evolves her own essence, and the reasons which she contains. And at first, indeed, she only, as it were, beholds herself, but when she penetrates more profoundly into the knowledge of herself, she finds in herself both Intellect (*Nous*) and the Orders of Beings. But when she proceeds into her interior recesses and into the adytum of the Soul, she perceives, with her eyes nearly closed, the Genus of the Gods and the Unities of Real Beings. For all things are potentially inherent in her according to the Soul's own characteristic, and through this we are naturally capable of knowing all things, by the inspiration of the powers and ideas of wholes which we contain."—*(Proclus on First Alcibiades)*

CXVI. "Explore thou the channel of the Soul, whence she cometh, and by what means, when she hath become a slave of the body, thou mayst again restore her to the order from which thou didst draw her, by uniting action with sacred word (logos)."

The eyes of the Soul are her gnostic powers by which she comes to know herself as well as the natures that are prior and posterior to herself; they are primarily threefold: noeric or spiritual and intellectual; dianoetic or rational and discursive; doxastic or opinionative and judicial.

"The one salvation of the Soul herself, which is extended by the Demiurgus and which liberates her from the circle of generation, from abundant wandering, and from an inefficacious life, is her return to the intellectual principle and a flight from everything which naturally adheres to her from generation. For it is necessary that the Soul, which descends like a seed into generation, should lay aside the stubble and bark, as it were, which she obtained from being disseminated into these fluctuating realms, and that, purifying herself from everything circumjacent, she should become an intellectual flower and fruit, delighting in an intellectual life instead of doxastic nutriment."—*(Proclus on "Timaeus")*

"The stronger Souls behold truth through themselves and are more inventive, being as the Oracle saith:

"CXVII. 'Saved through their own strength' "—*(Proclus in Alcibiades)*

"Plato considers Mathesis (instructional discipline) and Heuresis (invention or discovery) as paths of knowledge adapted to our Souls . . . the human Soul containing in herself all reasons and preassuming all sciences, is indeed darkened from generation respecting the theory of what it possesses, and requires discipline and invention; that through instructional discipline it may unfold its intellections and through invention may find itself and the plenitude of the inherent ideas or reasons. And these are the Gifts of the Gods, benefiting the Soul in its fallen condition and recalling it to an intellectual life."—*(ibid.)*

CXVIII. "For not by mortals whose thought is of body are things divine attainable, but they who stripped like athletes speed upwards to the height."

"Cathartic virtue alone must be called the salvation of souls, since this cuts off and vehemently obliterates material tendencies and the passions which adhere to us from generations, separates the Soul from body and leads it to intellect *(nous)*, causing it to leave on earth the vehicles with which it is invested."—*(Proclus on "Timaeus")*

In so far as the Soul is liberated from the bondage of the body, so it is said "to die" to the body, even while the body still lives; this, as Plato says in the Phaedo, is one of the great objects of the real philosopher, namely, "to study how to die and be dead".

CXIX. "The Souls of those who violently leave their bodies are most pure."

This mystical death is attained, as Olympiodorus declares: "by philosophizing in a manner truly cathartic".

Catharsis is purification or purgation from the attachments and defilements of material existence; it is the result of a telestic life, that is, one characterized by perfecting practices, sacred works, sacramental acts or ceremonies and rites.

"The telestic life, through the divine fire, causes all the defilements due to generation to disappear, as the Oracle teaches, and everything of an alien and irrational nature which the life of the Soul has attracted to itself."—*(Proclus in "Timaeus")*

"Sacred rites do not permit us to feed on seeds which decline towards the earth: for the earth is the last of things into which evil, according to Plato, being impelled,

perpetually revolves, and the Gods in the Oracles everywhere denominate it 'dregs' and continually exhort us to
fly from thence . . .

"For in sacred rites it is well worth extending the will in
such wise that it may rise above the power of the body, and
may cheerfully endeavour to comply with the divine institutions; for this, indeed, is eminently conducive to the
safety of the Soul—to pay a much greater attention to
itself than to the salubrity of the body; and even the body,
though in a secret manner, will appear to receive, by this
means, greater and more wonderful advantages; for when
the Soul gives the whole of herself to the Gods, and wholly
delivers herself to the guidance of Superior Natures, to
purifying rites, and prior to these, divine institutions taking the lead, nothing further now prohibiting and imped-
ing (for all things are contained in the Gods and subsist
about them); when this is the case, the Divine Light will
immediately shine through the Soul. But in consequence
of her being thus deified, she translates a certain vigorous
strength into her connate life, which when included, as it
were, possesses dominion, and becomes, through this life,
the cause of safety to the body . . .

"And, indeed, the Oracles of the Gods testify to the truth
of these assertions when they declare that through purifying ceremonies, not the Soul only, but bodies themselves
become worthy of receiving much assistance and health:
for they say—

"CXX. 'Even the mortal vesture of bitter matter is by
this means preserved'."—*(Emp. Julian. Orat. Sovereign
Sun)*

Thus, by means of telestic practices the Soul has a
refined and subtle nature or vehicle, which persists even
beyond the life of the ordinary physical body, as such.

CXXI. "Nor shouldst thou leave the dregs of matter on

the precipice; the eidolon (subtle etheric body) also hath its part in the All-radiant Place."

The precipice is the terrestrial region; the All-radiant Place is the Solar World above the lunar sphere.

"So that the manifested vehicle (body) may through the visible movement of them receive its fitting care, and the more divine part of it may be invisibly purified, and be restored to its native inheritance, as one of the Oracles of the Gods declares:

"CXXII. 'Being drawn up by the aery, lunar, and solar rays'."—*(Proclus in "Timaeus")*

CXXIII. "For the spirit which she collected from the spheres attends her when she comes out of the solid body."

CXXIV. "Extending the fiery mind *(nous)* to the work of piety, thou shalt preserve thy flowing body also."

As the Soul's potentialities are actualized so these are the powers whereby it mounts upward in the Great Ascent, passing through purifications and initiations, and gaining ever fuller and fuller visions of Reality as it approaches perfective union with the Divine.

"The word teleté or perfective initiation, says Hermeas, was so denominated from rendering the Soul perfect. The Soul is potentially perfect, but here below it is divided, as it were, and not able wholly to energize all its powers. But it is necessary to know that teleté, muésis, and epopteia differ from each other. Teleté is analogous to that which is preparatory to perfection; but muésis, which is so called from closing the eyes, is more divine; for to close the eyes in initiation is no longer to receive by sense those divine mysteries, but to behold them with the pure Soul itself; and epopteia signifies to be established in and become a spectator of the mysteries."—*(Thomas Taylor)*

"Wherefore, the Gods exhort us not to look towards

Them before we are hedged round about by the powers of the Mysteries."—*(Proclus in Alcibiades)*

CXXV. "Thou shouldst not look upon them before thy body is perfected."

Because that which is impure attracts to itself that which is of a like nature, hence it is said that evil entities (called evil or terrestrial daemons in the Oracles) molest imperfect man when he strives to reach the Empyrean Realm.

CXXVI. "Ever do they allure men's souls and lead them away from the Mysteries."

"And indeed, as to the theophanies and the life of the Mysteries, this is that which makes the ascent safe and steady, namely, the going forward in an orderly manner. Moreover, as the Oracle also says:

"CXXVII. 'For no other cause is the Face of God turned away from man and by His living power doth He send him on vain paths'—

"As when we make ascent to the most divine contemplations, or works, in a disorderly and inharmonious manner, and, as it is said, with profane lips and unwashen feet; for of those who thus approach the mysteries, imperfect is the passage, vain are their aspirations, and dark their paths."—*(Proclus on Parmenides)*

CXXVIII. "Behold thyself and tremble."

The more man knows his real Self the more is he inspired with true reverential awe in the presence of the Holy One.

CXXIX. "Believe thyself to be out of body and thou art."

But by supernatural faith the true mystic "loses himself" and plunges into the Divine Darkness which is before the Pavilions of God.

CXXX. "Even our ills sprout in us by our own will, for they are born from the nature of the life we lead."

They are the veils before the eyes of the Soul which obscure the Dazzling Radiance of the Divine Light.

CXXXI. "Seek Paradise."

"The Chaldaic Paradise is the Choir of Divine Powers about the Father of the Universe and the Empyrean Beauties of the Demiurgic Fountains."—*(Thomas Taylor)*

CXXXII. "Stain not Spirit, deepen not the plane."

The "Spirit" here is the "breath" or aerial nature of the Soul; the "plane" or superfices, refers to the Soul's differentiations, of an etherial and akashic nature, in the realms of time and space.

"For this principle of 'spirit' in the Soul, which the Blessed Ones call the spiritual Soul, becomes both divine and an all-various daemon and an image-body (eidolon), and in this the Soul atones for its misdeeds. The Oracles agree on this, for they compare the life of the Soul there (in Hades) to the fantastic visions of a dream."—*(Synesius)*

The hosts of the celestial Angels and Daemons assist the Soul when it aspires to climb the Blessed Mountain of the Gods; even as the terrestrial powers minister to man's mundane needs and thus seem to delay his progress by the worldly goods that man accumulates.

CXXXIII. "But when thou shalt behold a terrestrial daemon approaching make offering with invocation of the stone Mnuziris."

"Terrestrial daemons," says Taylor, "are full of deceit, as being remote from divine knowledge and replete with dark matter; he, therefore, who desires to receive any true information from one of these, must prepare an altar and sacrifice the stone Mnuziris, which has the power of causing another greater daemon to appear, who, approaching invisible to the terrestrial daemon, will give a true answer to the proposed question, and this to the interrogator himself."—*(Thomas Taylor)*

This refers to the power of sacred sympathy in telestic concerns and should be understood in a figurative rather than literal sense as indicative of the necessity of directing the mind to that which is celestial rather than terrestrial, for "The mind touches that which it thinks upon".

CXXXIV. "The Choir of Angels leads up the Soul in a certain manner, appearing about the Soul and causing her to be full of pure fire, thereby imparting to her stable order and power."

In the Soul's mystical ascent it can be conceived as passing upwards and outwards through the various worlds that are unfolded in the Chaldean Cosmology—the Zonic, the Azonic, and the Hyperzonic; thus, first it rises superior to the Zonic world with its sublunary and planetary spheres and wins the freedom of the inerratic sphere; secondly, it gains the liberty of the Azonic Realm, communing with the Angelic Hosts, freed from all the zones of Nature; and thirdly, it attains the Hyperzonic World and enters into more and more intimate relations with the Ruling, Vivific, and Solar Principles and the Gods who symbolize these divine principles, such as Apollo, Minerva, and Diana or Hecate. Thus, from Apollo comes the "Sounding Light" of the Spiritual Sun; from Minerva comes the power of true virtue and supernal excellence; from Hecate comes the secret of life and victory over death.

"Wherefore the Oracle saith that the ascending Souls sing a paean."—*(Olympiodorus)*

CXXXV. "The Soul breaks forth into hymns about divine things."

The paean was the measure especially associated with Apollo: it was stately and dignified, and is appropriate to the Soul's ascent from diversity to unity.

Such a Soul is truly inspired, and, with the Angelic choirs, sings the praises of the All-Father.

CXXXVI. "Alive in power he runs as an Angel."

"But the Souls of Theurgists, as Plato says, do not always remain in the Intelligible Realm, but they also descend into generation, concerning whom the Oracle says:

"Let fiery hope nourish thee

"CXXXVII. 'In the angelic region.' "—*(Proclus and Olympiodorus)*

"They (the Oracles) make the Soul descend often into the world either through losing her wings or through the Will of the Father."—*(Psellus)*

"But the Souls that live according to virtue shall, in other respects, be happy, and when separated from the irrational nature and purified from body, shall be conjoined with the Gods and govern the whole world, together with the Deities by Whom it was produced.

"And, indeed, though nothing of this kind should happen to the Soul, yet virtue herself, and the happiness and glory resulting from virtue, together with a life free from sorrow and subjection to others, would be sufficient to produce felicity in those who choose, and are able to pursue, a life wholly conformable to virtue itself."—*(Sallust on the Gods and the World)*

For the fiery breath of angelic inspiration enters the Soul that is purified from unworthy passions.

CXXXVIII. "Lightening her with the warmth of the spirit."

CXXXIX. "That which the Soul projects is easy to dissolve when it is revivified."

That is, when it is breathed into by "the warmth of the spirit".

The Oracles also speak of

CXL. "The earth from which it is necessary to lighten the heart"—from earthly things that weigh it down.

CXLI. "Quench not thy heart."

For even as the mind is illuminated by the Light of Apollo, so must the heart be warmed and expanded by the Divine Virtue and Wisdom of Minerva.

CXLII. "Clad in the full armour of the strength of the Sounding Light, arming both mind and soul with three-barbed might, thou must set in thy heart the whole symbol of the Triad, nor wander dispersedly on the fiery ways, but advance with steadfast tread."

CXLIII. "For verily fully-armed and arrayed for battle like unto the Goddess" (Minerva).

"We must show what the armour, and shields, and the spears are, and how these are antecedently comprehended in the Goddess Minerva ... The divine Iamblichus explains these in an inspired manner, he says: that shields are powers through which a divine nature remains impassive and undefiled, surrounding itself with an infrangible guard; but spears are the powers according to which it proceeds through all things in an exempt manner, and operates on all things, cutting off that which is material and giving aid to every genesiurgic form. These powers, however, are first seen about Minerva, and she is represented in armour, with spear and shield, for she vanquishes all things, and, according to the theologists, remains without declination and with undefiled purity in her father (Jupiter). . . . In Minerval Souls, the shield is the untamed and uninclining power of reason, but the spear is that power which amputates matter and liberates the Soul from fatal passions."—*(Proclus in "Timaeus".)*

CXLIV. "Urging thyself towards the centre of the Sounding Light."
"Apollo, subsisting as the principle of the choir of the Muses, which are around him, is—

"CXLV. 'A harmony of exultant light.' "—*(Proclus in "Cratylus".)*
"The Theurgist who presides over the mystic rites of Apollo, begins his operations from purifications and sprinklings."—*(Thomas Taylor)*

CXLVI. "First let the priest himself, who presides at the fiery works, be sprinkled with the cold water of the deep-sounding brine."
By such sacred oblations the Soul is lustrated and made pure to enter into communion with Divine Natures.

CXLVII. "Never change the native names, for there are in all languages God-given names which have ineffable power in the Mysteries."—*(Psellus)*
"As the theurgic art, through certain symbols, calls forth the unenvying Goodness of the Gods, in the same manner, the intellectual science of divine concerns, through compositions and divisions of sounds, exhibits the occult essence of the Gods. With great propriety, therefore, does Socrates in the Philebus assert that he proceeds with the greatest awe in that which respects the names of the Gods: for it is necessary to venerate the last resounding echoes, as it were, of the Gods, and in consequence of this reverence to maintain them in their first exemplars."—*(Proclus in "Theol. of Plato")*

But all the Gods are Aspects of the One God, and must be worshipped as such, and not idolatrously.

"Wherefore the Gods exhort us to understand—

"CXLVIII. 'The form of the Light which They display.'—(*Proclus in "Cratylus".*)

"For subsisting on high without form it (the light) becomes invested with form through its progression, and there being established, occultly and uniformly, it becomes apparent to us through the influence of the Gods; possessing indeed an efficacious energy through a divine cause, but becoming figured through the essence by which it is received."—(*ibid.*)

CXLIX.   "Energize about the Strophalos of Hecate."

The Strophalos, which was a revolving sphere of gold with a sapphire in the middle, was a sacred symbol in the Chaldean Mysteries, which referred to the Great World Mother and the Providential Life of which She is the source.

CL. "For Her hair appears to scintillate with sharp points of light."

This also, according to Proclus, refers to the Mater Deorum, Rhea-Hecate.

CLI. "The Soul of those who have speech will clasp God to herself: having nothing mortal she is wholly intoxicated with God."

CLII. "To some He granted to receive by instruction the Token of the Light, while to others even while asleep He gave the enjoyment of His strength."

"The Demiurgus of the universe impressed these symbols (or tokens) in Souls, by which they might be able

to abide in themselves and again convert themselves
to the sources of their being; and through the symbol
of unity, indeed, He conferred on them stability, but
through intellect, He imparted to them the power of
conversion."

But to this conversion, prayer is of the greatest utility;
for it attracts to itself the beneficence of the Gods, through
those ineffable symbols which the Father of Souls has
disseminated in them . . .

To a perfect and true prayer, however, there is
required, in the first place, a knowledge of the Divine
Orders to whom he who prays approaches, for no one
will accede to the Gods in a proper manner unless he
has a knowledge of Their natures. Hence the Oracle
admonishes:

"CLIII. That 'the fire-warmed conception' has the first
rank in sacred worship.

"But in the second place there is required a conforma-
tion of our life with that which is divine, accompanied by
all purity, discipline, and order, through which, our concerns being introduced to the Gods, we shall invite Their
beneficence and our Souls will become subject to Them; in
the third place, contact or communion is necessary,
according to which we touch the divine essence with
the summit (hyparxis) of our Soul and verge to a union
with it.

"But there is yet further required, an approximate
adhesion, for thus the Oracle calls it when it says:

"CLIV. 'For the mortal who approacheth the fire shall
have light from God.' "

"The Soul when thus converted to herself, finds symbols
of the Gods in all things—even the smallest—and through
these renders everything familiar and allied to the
Gods."—(*Proclus in "Timaeus".*)

CLV. "For the persevering mortal the Blessed Ones come swiftly into being"; but—

CLVI. "A mortal sluggish in these things spells dismissal of the Gods."

"The GOOD can only be known by a divine projection of the summit of the Soul, a projection of that which is above intellect, and which Plato calls the ray of the Soul, and says that the Soul inclining this ray should project herself to the GOOD through an oblation of all things posterior to it . . .

"As man is a microcosm, this ray of the Soul will be analogous to Truth or the Superessential Light in the Intelligible World, will be the summit of the Soul and that which the Platonists very properly call *the one* and the flower of our nature, for it is an illumination from the Ineffable Principle of all things."—(*Thomas Taylor on "Republic"*)

CLVII. "But the end of such ascents is the enjoyment of divine fruits and the filling of her up with self-radiant fire."

And thus does human emptiness become changed into the divine fullness or pleroma.

CLVIII. "Thou shalt behold a fire extending with leaping flashes through the waves of the air, or a fire without form whence a Voice proceedeth, or a rich light, all-splendid, whirling and circling with a mighty sound. Moreover, thou shalt behold a horse full of flashing light, or a boy riding upon a swift horse, all-flaming, or robed in gold, or naked, or shooting with a bow, or standing on the horse's back."

CLIX. "If Thou dost often commune with Me, thou shalt behold all things grow dark, then doth the curved immensity of heaven vanish, the stars shine not, the moon's light is veiled, the earth is shaken, and all things are thunderously aflame with lightning."

CLX. "But when Thou shalt behold a Sacred Fire without form shining with leaping flashes through the depths of the whole cosmos, HEAR THE VOICE OF THE FIRE."

'That which Nature binds, Nature also dissolves: and that which the soul binds, the soul likewise dissolves. Nature, indeed, bound the body to the soul; But the soul binds herself to the body. Nature, therefore, liberates the body from the soul; but the soul liberates herself from the body. Hence there is a twofold death; the one, indeed, universally known, in which the body is liberated from the soul; but the other peculiar to Philosophers, in which the soul is liberated from the body. Nor does the one entirely follow the other.'   *Porphyry*

'Happy he who mounts at length on wings of spirit and gazes on Depth Divine! It is toilsome to raise oneself on high; yet make firm the impulse, and the Sire will be at hand to aid. A ray of light will shine upon thy path, and show the Plain of Spirit. Come, my Soul, supplicate the Sire, abandon earth, mount up, and – united to God – dance as God thyself!'   *Synesius.*

Excerpts from the Commentary of Proclus on the Chaldean Oracles*

I. The eternal orders are the courts and dwelling-places of the Gods, and the paternal order is the *all-receiving abode of the Father*, which receives and unites all the souls that are borne upwards. But *the order of the Angels leads up the soul in a certain manner, appearing*, the Oracle says, *about the soul*, that is, shining upon her from every side and *causing her to be full of pure fire, thereby imparting to her a stable order and power*, through which she is not hurled forth into the disorder of matter, but is united to the light of the Gods; this moreover holds her in her native home and makes her to be unmixed with matter, *lightening her with the warmth of the spirit*, and raising her on high through the anagogic life. For *the warmth of the spirit* is participation in life; and all that hastens to the regions above is lightened, just as that which verges to matter becomes heavy. But *the end of such ascents is the enjoyment of divine fruits and the filling of her up with self-radiant fire*, and this is the contemplation of God, since it places her before the Eyes of the Father. And *the Soul* being perfected *breaks forth into hymns about divine things*, according to the Oracle, having before her and offering to the Father the ineffable tokens which the

* These Excerpts are all that remains of the ten books of the original work. In this Commentary there are several fragments of the Oracles which have not yet been quoted, but those which have already been given are well worth repetition, especially in the setting given to them by Proclus. The fragments are printed in italics.

Father placed in her in the first going-forth of being. For
such are the noeric and invisible hymns of the ascending
soul, which arouse in her the memory of the harmonious
reasons (logoi or words), which bear inexpressible images
of the divine powers which are in her.

II. The *depth of the Soul* means her triple gnostic
powers: noeric, dianoetic, and doxastic; and *all thine eyes*
her triple gnostic energies. For the eye is the symbol of
knowledge, but life of appetency, and both are triple. But
the earth, *from which it is necessary to lighten the heart*,
signifies all material and changing things existing in
generation, and all corporeal form. There follows *the contemplation of the Paternal Monad*, wherein is *pure joy and
tranquillity* from this noeric vision. From which it is clear
that the good is mingled from noeric contemplation
(noesis) and the joy which accompanies it. For all life,
having an energy of its own which is easily liberated,
enjoys a pleasure corresponding to it.

The *hymn of the Father* does not consist of compositions
or words nor anything laboriously prepared. For since He
alone is incorruptible, He does not receive a corruptible
hymn. Let us not therefore hope to persuade by some new
hurricane of syllables the Lord of True Words, nor by a
parade of artificially embellished actions. For God loves
unadorned beauty. Let this therefore be the hymn which
we dedicate, that of becoming like Him; let us leave
behind earth and its fluctuating existence; let us come to
the true goal. Let us know our Lord; let us love the Father;
let us obey Him Who calls us. Let us run towards the
warmth and escape from the cold. Let us become fire, and
journey through fire. We have an easy path for our ascent:
the Father guides us, revealing the fiery ways; let us not
flow from Lethe, a lowly stream.

III. The *root of evil* is the body, just as that of virtue is the mind (nous). For virtue blossoms out for souls from above, but evil forces its way in from worse natures and from below. But to *hurl it down to earth* is to cut it out of ourselves, and to enable the soul to ascend to her native order. She is allotted in matter to the order of generation, since evils necessarily circulate here and about this region. But our body also is a part of generation, and indeed it is possible to make a part of it unconquerable, but to do this to the whole of generation is impossible, unless we take away its very essence. Into generation, therefore, we must cast down *jealousy and envy*, whence the soul gathered them. For since they are of a material nature they have Matter (Hyle) for nurse. And the *quench not thy heart* with its tendency to descend to the Below does not mean merely rendering this invisible, as passions which are damped down within are wholly contained in any being and fill it with their own heat. But instead of quenching it, cast it out, and do not keep it dammed up within. Wherefore it adds: *Stain not spirit* through having envy within and concealing it. For *envy* is of a hylic nature. It accompanies a deprivation of goods; and deprivation has its subsistence in unproductive matter. But the race of mystics (theurgists) is free from envy, and zealously exerts itself in imitation of Divine Goodness, nor is it dragged down to the contentiousness and enmity of men. But these passions shut up in souls impart to the spirit a certain material quality of baseness, and qualify it with material deprivation and lifelessness.

IV. *When the soul lives* according to her dianoetic nature, she has the power to know that which is; but when she has established herself in the intellectual (noeric) part of her own essence she knows all things by simple and impartible intuitions. Ascending to The One, and folding up all the multitude in herself, she energizes in a divinely inspired manner and is united with the hyparxes which are beyond mind (nous). For everywhere like is naturally assimilated to like. And all knowledge binds the knower to the known by similitude; sense-perception to the sensible, dianoia to the objects of reasoning, and noesis to the intelligible. And in like manner *the flower of the mind* to that which is prior to intellect. For as in other things intellect is not the highest, but the cause beyond intellect, so in souls the first form of energy is not intellectual but more divine than intellect. And every soul and every intellect has two energies: first the unitary and that which transcends intuition (noesis), and second the noetic. It is necessary therefore to know That Intelligible as it subsists in itself and at its hyparxis by closing our eyes to all other lives and powers. For just as by becoming intellectual in nature we approach to intellect, so being unitary we leap up to union, standing upon the very summit of intellect, since even the eye does not see the sun except by becoming sun-like in form, and not by the light from a fire. Wherefore it is clear that that kind of knowing is unknowing. *But if*, the Oracle says, *thou dost force thy intellect within*: that is to say, that if you put the weight of intellectual assaults into the attempt to contact It *and thus knowest That Intelligible, as knowing some one thing*, that is, according to some measure of form and knowledge which requires attention—if thus, *That thou shalt not know*. For even though such intellections (noesis) may be simple, they fall short of the single simplicity of the intelligible, and are projected into secondary intellectual natures, thus already coming forth into multitude. For nothing knowable is known by a gnostic faculty inferior to itself. That, therefore, which is beyond mind (nous) is not to be known through mind. For immediately mind gives its attention to a certain thing, it pronounces that thing to be the object of intellection (noumenon), and by this very act is secondary to the intelligible. But if it is with the flower of the mind (nous) which is within us that we know This

Intelligible, which is established at the summit of the First Intelligible Triad, by what is it that we are united with The One who is exempt from all things and imparticipable? For if the First Father is said *immediately to withdraw Himself from Mind and Power*, Who is He that needs not thus to withdraw Himself, but is completely and utterly withdrawn from all things, and is celebrated as the *God of all*? But is not this elsewhere also said of the First Father of all? And *the First Power of the Sacred Word (Logos)*—Who is He that is beyond this, and of Whom this First Power participates, and thereby is said to be *sacred*? And if He that manifests That which is more ineffable is named a *Word (Logos)*, it is necessary that prior to the Word there should be *the Silence* which is the hypostasis of the Word, and prior to everything sacred the deific cause. As therefore the things which are posterior to the intelligibles are "Words" (logoi or reasons) of the intelligibles, when they (the intelligibles) are united, so the "word" which is in the intelligibles themselves, subsisting from another more ineffable unity, is a word of the Silence which is prior to the intelligibles, but a Silence of the silent intelligibles. It cannot be therefore that *the flower of the mind* and the flower of our whole soul are the same thing. But the one is that which is most uniform in our intellectual life, but the other is the inity of all the powers of the soul, which latter are multiform. For we are not mind (nous) alone; but reason (dianoia) and opinion (doxa) and attention and freewill, and, prior to these faculties, an essence both one and manifold, partible and impartible. And the one, in manifesting, becomes twofold, and one of these principles is the flower of the first of all our powers, but the other is the centre of our whole being and of all the manifold powers about this centre. But of these the former alone unites us to the Father of the Intelligibles. For one is intellectual, and that too is known by the Mind of the Father, according to the One which is in It; but the one

towards which all the powers of the soul converge can by
its nature only lead us towards That which is beyond all
things that are, and is itself that which brings into unity
all that is in us. So that we are rooted in That by our
essence, and, through being so rooted, even if we proceed
from It, we shall not alienate ourselves from our cause.

V. Philosophy ascribes the departure from the Gods to
a forgetfulness of the eternal words (logoi), and the return
to Them to the remembrance of these, but the Oracles
speak of the *tokens of the Father*. And both of these agree.
For the soul subsists from the intellectual (noeric)
"Words" (logoi) and the divine symbols, of which the
former are from the intellectual ideas, but the latter from
the divine unities. And we are likenesses of intellectual
natures, but statues of unknown tokens. And just as every
soul is a pleroma of all types, but subsists as a wholeness
according to one, so also it participates of all the tokens
through which it is united to divine things, but its hyparxis is distinguished by one, so that all the multitude which
is in it is gathered up into one summit. For it is necessary
to know this also—that every soul differs according to its
type from every other soul, and that there are as many
types of souls as there are souls. For there is first a subsistence of many indivisible uniform natures according to
one type (distributed) about matter and the components of
things, the one substanding nature participating vari-
ously of the same form; secondly, the being of the soul is a
word (or reason), and a pure type; wherefore a soul will
either differ according to its essence in no respect from any
other, or it will differ according to its type. For this is the
only thing which will differ: it is type alone. Whence it is
clear that every soul, even though it is filled with the same
reasons (logoi), yet is allotted one type distinct from the
rest, just as the solar type characterizes the solar soul, and
another type another.